WINDOW BOX AND
CONTAINER GARDENING

WINDOW BOX
AND
CONTAINER
GARDENING

JUDITH BERRISFORD

FABER AND FABER, LONDON

First published in 1974
by Faber and Faber Limited
3 Queen Square London WC1
Printed in Great Britain by
Butler & Tanner Ltd,
Frome and London

ISBN 0 571 10113 5

Contents

CONTENTS

*Part Three: Window box and container gardening in
warmer climates*

6

Illustrations

7

16. a. Old wheelbarrows make interesting containers
b. Plastic lining containers help to keep up a succession
of interest

Line drawings

Acknowledgments

I should like to thank my husband, Cliff Lewis, for his unfailing patience and help in all my garden exploits; Miss Eileen Brooksbank of Faber for encouraging me to write about them and—as garden editor—being an example of what all good publishers should be to their authors, a source of ready and constructive criticism and support; Miss Ann Bonar, for her valuable advice and conscientious checking; my very good friend of longstanding, Miss Phyllis White, for taking many of the black and white photographs at my request and Mr Ernest Crowson and Mr Harry Smith for supplying the others from their extensive collections of beautiful prints. Mr Smith also provided the colour photographs.

I should like to thank, too, my garden-friends of both hemispheres for the interest and zest they have given to our visits and conversations over the years—especially those who have attended my slide-talks aboard ships and joined in the enthusiastic discussions afterwards—also the directors and staff of Union-Castle, British India, P. & O. and Royal Mail lines who have made my shipboard lectures possible and enabled me to travel so extensively as to effectively widen the scope of my knowledge and ideas.

J. M. B.

Foreword

As travel writers and shipboard lecturers, as well as enthusiastic gardeners, my husband and I have visited many parts of the world. We have spent long periods in South Africa, New Zealand, Madeira and the Canary Isles and as keen gardeners have enjoyed seeing many of the plants we grow in British gardens growing in the wild. We have become accustomed to the many cultivated subjects that do well outdoors in climates warmer than our own and have studied garden conditions and become familiar with garden methods and the expediences of garden design in countries in other latitudes.

Always keen on window box and container gardening, we have paid particular attention, during our travels, to this facet of the art and in this book I am aiming to help gardeners abroad as well as at home with notes on container design and construction, plants, composts, propagation, cultivation and the combating of pests and diseases.

Part Three is devoted to window box and container gardening in warm climates and in the southern hemisphere but overseas gardeners will find their problems discussed and their conditions borne in mind throughout the various chapters in the book.

Judith Berrisford
   Deganwy, North Wales,
   Fish Hoek, Cape Province,
    Republic of South Africa,
     and
   Takapuna, Auckland,
   New Zealand.

Introduction

Window boxes and containers have an increasing part to play in modern gardening, being able completely to transform a bleak wall or a plain house front. Not only may they be used to decorate town-houses and garden-less flats and offices, but they have a very real function in providing additional places to grow flowers wherever the garden area is restricted.

Such present-day small gardens (as are to be found on the numerous housing estates on the outskirts of every town and many villages) have little room for mass colour. Indeed, in such gardens, the use of bedding displays can create a harsh and restless effect.

It is far better to give the garden a framework of evergreens, within which borders and bays of small ornamental shrubs, roses, bulbs and perennials provide flowers in seasonal succession around such focal points as a lawn, paved area or pool. This will give a restful and dignified overall effect against which the massed colour of window boxes, troughs and urns provides interest and eye-appeal, enhancing and beautifying the house and its surroundings without detracting from the peace and naturalness of the garden.

In this respect, American, New Zealand, Australian and South African gardens have the edge over their British counterparts. In these countries, as in much of France, Germany and Switzerland and northern Italy, the use of greenery in the garden scheme is

13

well understood. Perhaps the hotter summer sun leads to an appreciation of cool effects. The consequent drier conditions ensure the appreciation of ground cover to trap dust and conserve moisture, while trees and shrubs are necessary both to provide shade and to rest the eye.

Auckland, Durban and Los Angeles come at once to mind as cities in which even the smallest suburban gardens have this quality of dignity and peace. They have their window boxes and containers, too, fronting the sun-decks and flanking the stoeps. Urns stand beside the swimming pools, olive-oil jars and pots supply colour for patios and terraces.

Recently, in Britain, the use of window boxes and containers has been more widely appreciated. Numerous modern bungalows have deep window boxes and troughs of tongued and grooved teak or cedar provided by the builder. Other householders make their own or buy antique reproductions in fibre glass or pre-cast stone.

Most garden-supply shops stock plastic troughs in green or white intended to be used as jardinières or to stand on inside window ledges, and I have seen these used as outside window boxes, but they are not really suitable. They are apt to be shallow, can be blown off the sills in a heavy wind and at best are only satisfactory for the smaller bedding plants such as lobelia or nemesia. They are useful, though, as linings (stocked with heathers for winter, hyacinths for spring, French marigolds and lobelia or miniature dahlias for summer and autumn) to change and replenish permanent boxes. In this case, drainage is very important and where the lining troughs have no drainage holes the plants should be grown in Levington compost with extra charcoal added to keep it sweet.

Deep boxes and troughs are useful to grow the larger permanent plants such as evergreen azaleas, camellias or hydrangeas. By the addition of bulbs, heaths or an interplanting of pelargoniums (geraniums) these can be made to supply colour almost all the year round.

When choosing window boxes and troughs to front sun-decks or balconies, consideration must be given to the style of the house.

Antique reproductions look right with Regency and Georgian buildings but fussy and disastrous with modern bungalow designs. Bark-fronted rustic boxes suit a cottage in the country and can be pleasant and in keeping with small terraced or semi-detached houses in country areas, but they would look quite out of place with stucco or Portland stone.

For 18 months, shortly after we were married, a business move caused my husband and I temporarily to abandon a large house and 16-acre garden for a mini-semi in the Cleveleys area of Blackpool where we had only a small paved plot at the rear of the house. Pocket-handkerchief in area, it lay between the garage and wash-house, and had a close-boarded wooden fence at the side and back. When we moved there, the only growing thing was a standard 'Grenadier' apple tree.

Used to large country gardens, we craved plants and flowers. My husband bought a large coal-bunker barrel which he painted green and on the top of which we stood a shallow circular container, in which we planted ivy-leafed perlargoniums to trail down the sides. We built a raised bed over the roots of the apple tree, set it with nasturtium seeds and filled it with a riot of cream and lemon and flame. Four vinegar barrels were scrubbed and charred (see p. 83), filled with soil and used as containers for hydrangeas to stand on the paving. A fifth became a water-garden in a tub. My husband hacked three small beds in the paving so that we could grow delphiniums against the garage wall. Against the side fence he built a raised box-bed edged with bricks in which we could grow bulbs and Brompton stocks with autumn-sown sweetpeas trained to cover the boarding. The back fence was treated in a similar way with antirrhinums as foreground to a drapery of scarlet runner beans. We fitted boxes to the window ledges of the garage, wash-house and house. Fronted with bark, these were entirely suitable to their setting and afforded homes in turn to blue and lemon polyanthus interplanted with muscari, to white and lavender violas and late-summer antirrhinums.

However restricted one's surroundings, it is often possible by using window boxes and containers to have the supreme enjoyment of growing flowers—and not only flowers, because many housewives supplement their range of culinary flavourings by raising herbs in a kitchen window box.

The function of window boxes and containers is, then, three-fold. They afford a means of growing plants where no garden exists, and they embellish the outside of buildings by their own presence in conjunction with the flowers and foliage they house. In addition they allow striking colour effects to be added without interfering with the garden design.

Although cedar and teak are now being used for window boxes, many are still made of plain wood, painted to match or contrast with the colour of the house. White or cream window boxes look well with almost any building style and are particularly suitable in countries with hot summer climates because white and cream are colours that reduce the amount of heat absorption and so keep the soil cool. Pale blue, grey, and green are popular, while yellow gives a sunny effect against a white or stone-coloured background. When choosing the colour of the boxes, it is important to visua-lise them planted with the kind of flowers you want to grow. Pale blue is charming when planted with rose, yellow or orange flowered plants. Deep blue makes choice more difficult. Yellow clashes with pink. Even different shades of green can sometimes strike a jarring note. White, cream and grey are undoubtedly the easiest to suit but black can look smart and is particularly suitable with black and white half-timbered houses.

Window boxes are usually little more than 8 or 9 inches deep, so they can be used only for plants which will grow readily in about 7 inches of soil. This limits the plantings to the smaller bulbs; shallow-rooted perennials such as polyanthus primroses, pansies and herbs; bedding plants like petunias, ivy-leafed pelar-goniums, antirrhinums and marigolds and such small shrubby subjects as winter-flowering heathers (*Erica carnea*), periwinkle (*Vinca minor*), dwarf hebes (veronica) and fuchsias.

In order to grow even temporary plants successfully in window boxes there must be adequate drainage. A suitable compost or good, friable loam must be chosen, and the growing medium should be changed every two years.

Even more important, when dealing with upper-storey decorations, the window box must be firmly fixed in position so that it cannot fall and cause possible injury to passers-by. For a similar reason, if the window box overhangs the street, an anti-drip device must be fitted to take care of surplus water.

These important facets, together with window box and container construction and variety and choice of plants for different aspects, will be dealt with in subsequent chapters.

PART ONE

Window Boxes

A striking summer window box planted with Petunias, zonal
Pelargoniums, Marguerites and *Lysimachia nummularia*
(Creeping Jenny)

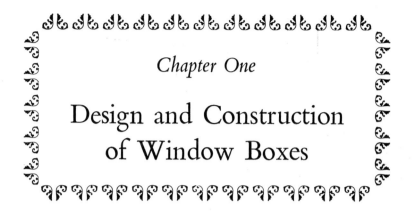

Conditions governing window box design are apt to differ from house to house and to vary with the requirement of individual gardeners so—as they are comparatively simple for a carpenter or home-handyman to construct—it is as well to have them 'tailor made' for their particular job.

Upper-storey boxes in particular *must* be fitted with a gutter to prevent drip. To encourage surplus water to drain into this gutter, the bottom of the box must slope slightly towards the front. A thin pipe should be connected to the gutter to lead the water down to a surface drain (Fig. 1). This pipe can be painted so that it merges into the brick, or roughcast or stonework of the house.

In cool climates, softwood or deal is the best material for painted window boxes, and it should be planed to about an inch thick, primed, and then painted inside and out with two under-coats and a top-coat of gloss, as much to preserve it as for the sake of appearance. For a more rustic effect, treatment with the various wood preservatives will prove satisfactory.

In hot countries, hardwoods such as teak give a better protection against borers and fungi. Length will be determined by the size of the window, but it is not generally wise to have boxes more than 4 feet long. Two boxes, each 3 feet long, will be found to be the best way of dealing with a window sill 6 feet wide. Otherwise the

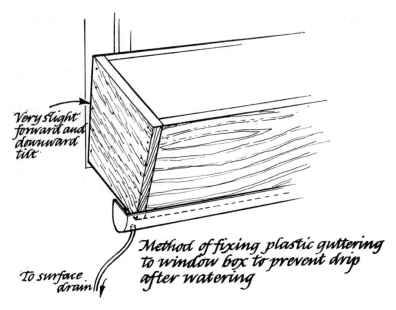

Very slight forward and downward tilt

To surface drain

Method of fixing plastic guttering to window box to prevent drip after watering

FIGURE 1.

boxes, when full of soil, become too heavy and almost impossible to handle—constituting a real danger if above ground-floor level.

For maximum effect the boxes should be 10–12 inches wide, giving room for a double row of staggered plants and allowing dwarf subjects such as pansies, lobelia, ageratum, winter heath or crocuses to be used as an edging. The boxes can be either square in section or can taper towards the wall at the bottom. The base, however, should not be less than 8 inches in width. The inside depth of the box should be at least 8 inches, allowing room for a 7-inch depth of compost.

For a really durable job, brass screws should be used in conjunction with synthetic resin adhesive, and the four sides secured to corner posts, each an inch square. Turn the box upside down to screw on the bottom. Then bore drainage holes an inch in diameter at intervals of about a foot along the central line of the bottom of the box.

Drying out is a problem on south-facing walls in this country and in the hot sun experienced in many countries abroad. To combat this, double-walled boxes can be made, using quarter-inch timber for the outer wall, and leaving half an inch of space between the two walls which can be packed with dry peat or dry sphagnum moss (Fig. 2). This method can be used also in Scan-

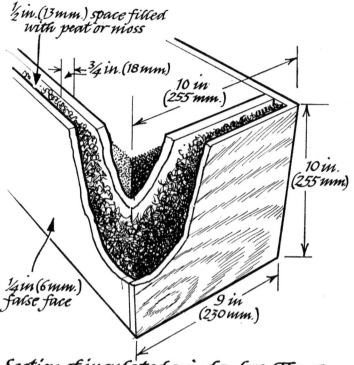

½ in. (13mm.) space filled with peat or moss

¾ in. (18mm)

10 in (255 mm.)

10 in. (255 mm.)

¼ in (6mm.) false face

9 in (230 mm.)

Section of insulated window box. The space between the two walls to be packed with dry peat or moss to prevent drying out in hot countries and to provide insulation in cold places

FIGURE 2.

dinavia, the South Island of New Zealand, and those parts of the United States which experience a severe winter, to enable spring bulbs to come through the winter frost unharmed. Even in the colder parts of Britain where it is desired to have a winter display of heaths or to have hyacinths ready for spring flowering, this method has much to recommend it.

Deeper boxes to fix in front of balcony or verandah rails may be made of two or three plain boards in horizontal juxtaposition.

Securing is important. All window boxes must be firmly fixed into position. With wooden window frames this can usually be done by screwing an angle bracket to the bottom of the box and to the window frame. With metal windows, special brackets may have to be made and professionally fixed into place. Where the sill slopes, wedge-shaped chocks of wood should be hammered into position to support the outer edge of the box and to keep it level. This also has the effect of raising the box off the sill and allowing surplus water to escape.

Where the window sills are too narrow it will be necessary to fix slanting brackets beneath the box to affix it to the wall and to give additional support.

Boxes that are deeper or wider have the advantage of being able to accommodate larger plants such as hydrangeas and regal pelargoniums, but they are more difficult to fix and require special ties put into the wall or a series of strong supporting brackets (Fig. 3). Such boxes, which form permanent additions to the house, should be tongued and grooved and made of teak. Vertically-grooved boxes, built in this fashion, are attractive and need only a yearly application of teak oil to keep them in good condition.

Such boxes are sometimes supported on metal stanchions, sunk into the paving beneath the window sill or accommodated in raised brick 'boxes'. Others have their own stands and, although capable of being placed on any paved area in the garden, are most attractive sited under a window. Self-supporting boxes prevent damage to the fabric of the building and have the advantage of being readily interchangeable.

Liners are advisable where long-lived subjects such as azaleas or hydrangeas are used to provide seasonal display. These can readily be purchased in plastic from most garden stores. If they are not provided with drainage, holes should be bored to coincide with the drainage holes in the actual window boxes. The plants can then be set in good compost and the containing troughs removed

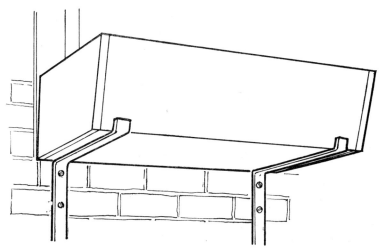

Method of fixing window-box by simple angle brackets with ends bent upwards to retain box

FIGURE 3.

to enable the plants to spend their dormant period in the shelter of a greenhouse or sun-porch. Where a heated greenhouse is available it pays dividends to have a series of interchangeable plastic troughs to use as liners for the window boxes. Plants can then be raised in these troughs, brought to the height of their display under glass, gradually hardened off and then placed in the boxes without root disturbance.

Some gardeners use their window boxes as jardinières, growing their plants in pots and packing the pots into the window boxes with peat. This allows a ready interchange of growing material, and is useful in conjunction with a greenhouse or cold frame.

Not all window box owners have these facilities, however, and for them the method of planting direct into the growing medium is the most satisfactory.

The finish of boxes is important and when thinking of window boxes we can take the term to include, also, window box types of container mounted on feet and used to adorn the narrow tile ledges at the base of hardwood panelling sometimes used to decorate the front aspect of a modern bungalow. Such boxes, vertically grooved and made of teak or cedar to match the facia panelling, can also be used outside verandah or balcony railings or beneath a loggia window. If used on a balcony or verandah, however, the additional precaution should be taken of wiring them into position against disturbance by cats or heavy wind.

Such boxes may also be constructed of plain horizontal wood boards and painted.

Plain wood boxes can be decorated (after painting to preserve the wood) with glued-on strips of varnished mahogany or laminated plastic offcuts. Regency-type mouldings for whitewood furniture may also be used and can be pleasing if painted white, cream or grey to match the boxes.

Wooden boxes and troughs can be given a stone finish by painting with PVA adhesive and sprinkling with river sand. When this dries, a thin layer of cement mortar mixed with equal parts of water and PVA adhesive should be trowelled on. This method gives a convincing stone appearance and can be used to transform plastic tubs and other containers in a similar way.

Corrugated asbestos may also be used for the front and sides of boxes, thus lessening the weight, and can look very effective when painted.

Outside plant holders to take the place of window boxes and provide homes for plants without putting the strain of heavy soil-filled boxes on the wall may be made from $1\frac{1}{2}$ by $1\frac{1}{2}$-inch softwood, brass-screwed and glued (with synthetic resin adhesive) into position. Construct a rectangular frame as shown in Fig. 4, leaving the openings just wide enough for the plant rims to rest on the divisions without falling through. This should be supported on three galvanised brackets, the length of which must be the same as the width of the frame in order to give adequate support. With the pots colour-washed to match the frame, and with trailers such as ivy used to alternate with the flowering plants, this can be most decorative in effect.

A comparatively new idea is the use of decorative wrought-iron work to form a protective framework to support and hold window boxes in position. This is particularly useful for town-houses

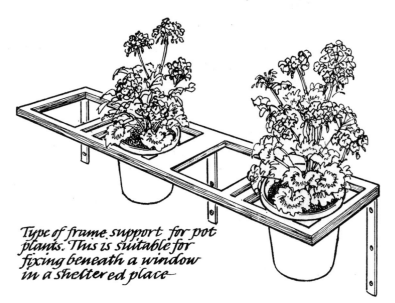

Type of frame support for pot plants. This is suitable for fixing beneath a window in a sheltered place

FIGURE 4.

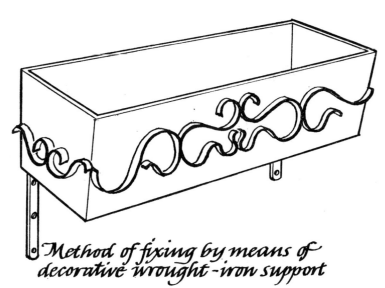

Method of fixing by means of decorative wrought-iron support

Figure 5.

27

as it enables one to use lightweight plastic troughs as containers, which the wrought-iron work will effectively disguise (Fig. 5).

Fibre glass boxes are light in weight and although more expensive are well worth consideration, especially where a graceful building deserves the dignity of an antique box such as may be provided by the authentic-looking fibre glass reproductions of sixteenth, seventeenth and eighteenth century lead boxes made by Verine, with classic designs in high relief. They are not cheap, a box 3 feet in length costing over £10 at the time of writing, but as permanently decorative additions to contribute to the exterior beauty of a house they are not an unreasonable proposition. Such boxes may best be supported by angle brackets pegged into the wall.

Chapter Two

Drainage and Composts

In window box gardening the regulation of drainage is one of the key factors in success. Obviously drainage holes should be provided wherever possible to prevent the soil becoming waterlogged and stagnant. Equally obviously the drainage must not be too sharp or the compost will very quickly dry out.

To this end, before filling the box with compost, each drainage hole should be covered with a flat stone or piece of broken crock with the curved side uppermost. Shallow boxes (with a depth of 10 inches or less) may be lined with black plastic sheeting in which drainage holes have been pierced to correspond with the holes in the bottom of the box. The flat stones or pieces of crock can then be placed inside the polythene to cover the holes.

Where the boxes are deep enough (15 inches or more in depth) put a thin layer of weathered ashes at the bottom, covered with oblongs of thin turf placed grass downwards. Where the depth of the box is between 10 and 15 inches sphagnum moss should be used instead of the turves. The growing medium is then added and pressed well down to leave a clear inch below the top of the box. (Fig. 6).

The actual compost serves several important functions, keeping the plants firmly in place and upright, providing an anchor for the roots and acting as a reservoir for plant foods, air and water.

For bedding plants used to decorate window boxes such as

pelargoniums, petunias, antirrhinums, etc. John Innes potting compost No. 2 or 3 will be adequate—with the proviso that the compost must be changed each spring. This, in any case, is usually necessary since the compost becomes full of roots and exhausted by the rapid growth and continued flowering of the plants.

Where bulbs or corms such as begonias are to be used I prefer a compost containing at least a third and preferably 75 per cent of moist peat so as to retain more moisture for the greater water need of the plants. Hydrangeas, too, as well as polyanthus primulas or

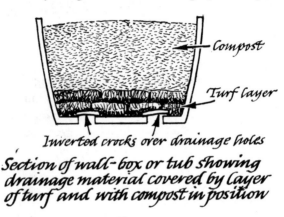

Section of wall-box or tub showing drainage material covered by layer of turf and with compost in position

Figure 6.

Primula denticulata for spring flowering, do better in a peaty compost. In places where the summers are hot such as the Mediterranean region, California, Australia, New Zealand and South Africa, the moisture-holding qualities of peat are essential. In these countries, it is worth constructing a double-skinned box as described in the previous chapter. The space between the two skins should be filled with moss, dry peat or chopped, rotted turves to insulate the box against the heat and to prevent drying out.

A good all-purpose compost may be made up of 3 parts peat to 1 of sand (parts by bulk). This, it will be realised, contains no plant food as such, so it will be necessary artificially to feed plants grown in this medium. A fertiliser with a fairly high nitrogen content such as John Innes Liquid Feed, Bio Plant Food or other proprietary fertiliser should be used.

Maxicrop, the seaweed fertiliser, also gives good results and is especially useful for shrubby subjects such as hydrangeas and heaths. Begonias also respond well.

John Innes liquid feed is made up of 15 parts by weight of ammonium sulphate, $2\frac{3}{4}$ parts potassium nitrate and $2\frac{1}{4}$ parts mono-ammonium phosphate, dissolved at the rate of $\frac{1}{2}$ oz of the mixture to a gallon of rain water and used fresh. It may also be used dry, as a topdressing if mixed with fine sand to act as a carrier.

Bio Plant Food is a useful, ready-made, concentrated, organic-based liquid fertiliser. It contains nitrogen, phosphates, potash and necessary trace elements. Diluted at 1 tablespoon to a gallon of water it should be used at fortnightly intervals.

A good compost is that recommended by the Royal Horti-cultural Society for the pot cultivation of camellias. It consists of 7 parts by bulk of turfy loam, 3 parts granulated sedge peat and 2 parts of gritty, lime-free sand. To each bushel should be added $1\frac{1}{2}$ oz of hoof and horn and $1\frac{1}{2}$ oz of bonemeal. Where pelargoniums and other lime-happy subjects are to be grown this may have a little ground limestone added. This compost is more suitable for strong growers such as azaleas, begonias, fuchsias and pelargoniums, and for permanently planted boxes and patio containers, than for small summer annuals such as French marigolds, ageratum, lobelia, alyssum, nasturtiums and the like, which, in Britain at any rate, do best in John Innes Compost No. 1 which can often be purchased ready mixed. John Innes No. 3 contains more fertilizer and chalk and is really better for long-term plantings of larger subjects.

Whatever compost one uses it is most important that it should be changed at least once every two years. Otherwise the compost at the bottom of the box may become stagnant and waterlogged. Also the feeds and fertilisers may result in toxic residues which must be removed.

Levington potting compost is suitable for window box en-thusiasts without gardens. This is a soil-less compost, based on peat and containing all the foods necessary to keep plants growing well for the first six weeks. From then on feed with Fisons Liquinure every 10 days.

The compost is available in waterproof plastic bags, in easily managed sizes, and being both odourless and entirely clean, is particularly suitable for office, flat, hotel and shop window boxes.

Levington potting compost, like all peat composts, must not be allowed to dry out but, on the other hand, it should not be allowed to become too wet. Should drying out unfortunately occur, water twice within a day to ensure the presence of moisture throughout the compost.

Plantgrow, marketed by Fisons, is an excellent compost for heavier plants requiring firm root anchorage.

Bio Humus is a mixture of organic matter, seaweed extract and chalk laced with nitrogen, phosphates, potash and trace elements. Half a pound of this product mixed into a 75 per cent peat/25 per cent sand compost will ensure good results from a window box 3 feet long and 9 or 10 inches deep.

Like Levington compost this is a good growing medium for convenience' sake, and a boon to those who have neither the facilities nor the time to prepare a more complicated mixture.

Watering—just as the provision of plant foods and the prevention of drying out are important factors leading to success with window boxes, so watering is also important. As a rule window boxes should not be allowed to become dry but in cool countries, in the early stages of establishing fibrous-rooted subjects such as petunias, French marigolds and zonal and ivy-leafed pelargoniums the judicious withholding of water can be beneficial.

The box should be well watered before planting and then allowed to become rather dry. This will ensure the root system of the plants extending in search of moisture and will result in thriving and vigorous masses of roots.

However, a careful watch must be kept on the boxes, and the plants given water as soon as they show signs of flagging.

Before applying a liquid fertiliser it is important to ensure that the compost is moist. With window boxes this means watering before each feed as a general rule.

During the first month after planting no additional fertiliser is needed, but thereafter a fortnightly liquid feed will be appreciated.

Some plants, especially nasturtiums and French marigolds, produce leaf at the expense of flower if they are given too much nutrient so they need only very sparing boosts of liquid feed. If grown in John Innes compost Nos. 2 or 3 containing John Innes base fertiliser they will not need any additional feeding.

Window boxes should be watered when the sun has gone off them for the day. It is better to give a good soaking that will keep the compost moist for several days rather than to give more frequent shallow waterings which will encourage surface rooting and so make the plants more susceptible to drought.

Holidays can present a problem to the window box enthusiast. So, where it is expected that periodic absences from home will render difficult systematic watering, it is worth considering covering the moistened compost with black polythene before planting. Crosses are cut in the polythene where the plants are to be inserted, and the flaps are then folded back to form planting circles.

Black polythene used in this way tends to make the compost more stagnant, so to offset this, additional charcoal should be added to the mixture.

The use of a polythene mulch for the window boxes will be found helpful, too, in hot countries and in office blocks with south-facing exposures where the plants have to remain untended over the weekends.

Living mulches in the form of ground-covering plant material help to reduce moisture loss as well as being decorative in their own right. They can be permanently planted at the back of window boxes or containers and allowed to find their own way to the light, covering the soil area as they go. The interchange of bedding plants in the boxes and the topping up of the compost is usually possible without disturbing them too much.

Selection of plant material is among the greatest pleasures of window box gardening. Particularly for spring is there a fascinating wealth of subjects from which to choose. Colour schemes, here, must be taken into account for one must use those plants whose flowers associate most harmoniously with both the window box and the background colour of the house. Yellow daffodils, for instance, would not look good in a blue-painted window box against a pink-washed wall yet a white variety such as the short and sturdy 'Mount Hood' would look charming, particularly if associated with trails of cream-splashed ivy such as *Hedera* 'Silver Queen' and with blue grape hyacinths, *Muscari* 'Heavenly Blue', at the front of the box.

Bulbs are particularly suitable for spring boxes and for the main display one should rely on the sturdy, long-lasting hyacinths. The flowers of the early double tulips also have a long-life span. Both of these subjects may be edged with crocuses—the very early *Crocus chrysanthus* varieties or the fat Dutch hybrids which flower later. Or one may plant alternate clumps of each to ensure a longer display. Snowdrops may be included for earliest bloom and will establish well in the garden afterwards if planted out while green and set beneath deciduous trees or at the forefront of shrubs. All window box bulbs should be given a second chance of usefulness, and those who have no garden in which to plant them may like to pass them on to more fortunate friends who will probably be glad to reciprocate by housing winter heaths or azaleas in their shady border during the summer months or by gifts of surplus plants for window box display.

Hyacinths need some sun and prefer south- or west-facing window boxes. They should be set 4 inches deep and 7 inches apart in October. 'Prepared' bulbs which have been subjected to special treatment to bring them into flower for Christmas need heat and are, of course, unsuitable for window boxes. The grade of bulb sold as 'bedding hyacinths' is right for the job as the heavier flower spikes of 'exhibition' bulbs are more likely to be snapped by the equinoctial gales that all too frequently make havoc of daffodils and narcissi in the garden beds and borders. Hyacinths for bedding are frequently sold by colour. Where they are offered by variety, the bright crimson 'Jan Bos', pale blue 'Myosotis', bright pink 'Ann Marie' and pale yellow 'City of Haarlem' are telling ones to choose.

Early double tulips last almost a month in flower but, offering more wind resistance than the hyacinths, should be used only for sheltered window boxes. Effective varieties are the blood-red 'Dante', 'Orange Nassau', 'Peach Blossom' and the canary yellow, orange-flushed 'Maréchal Niel'. They should be planted 3 inches deep and 4 inches apart, or may be set at a wider spacing and interplanted with polyanthus primulas.

Smaller bulbs may be used in association to give a long season of interest, and have a delightful spring-like effect. Suitable for inclusion would be the *Iris reticulata* 'Clairette' with Cambridge blue standards and Oxford blue falls; small, early daffodils such as 'February Gold', 'Peeping Tom' or 'March Sunshine' with the pretty little narcissus 'Beryl' with primrose perianth and a shallow orange crown; grape hyacinths (*Muscari*) in blue and white, starry, pale blue *Chionodoxa luciliae*, and daisy-petalled *Anemone blanda* in deep bright blue.

For sheltered boxes, pink May-flowering Darwin tulips such as 'Clara Butt' would be effective interplanted with late Pheasant's Eye narcissi.

To associate with bulbs and to drape the front of window boxes, aubrieta in mauve and purple can be very effective.

35

Specialised boxes that can give great pleasure may be planted with evergreen azaleas or dwarf rhododendrons. These may be set either in plastic liners or in individual pots, packed around with peat and sunk into the ground in a shady plot after flowering to wait until they are next required.

Small rhododendrons and evergreen azaleas are useful in that they furnish the boxes with their foliage during the winter as well as flowering beautifully in April and May. Earlier colour may be supplied by planting clumps of rock-garden crocuses and dwarf daffodils between the shrubs.

Of the rhododendrons the lilac R. *pemakoense* with airy funnel-shaped flowers is one of the best and freest to bloom. It looks charming in association with yellow primroses. It can be relied on to bloom freely each year, even as a very young plant.

Also in this category is the dwarf clone of R. 'Elizabeth'—R. 'Jenny'. This plant has the same bright scarlet-red, gloxinia-shaped trumpets as its parent. Its small leaves are dark and pointed and its habit is low and mounded, remaining under a foot in height. It is pretty in association with the clear blue periwinkle, *Vinca minor* 'La Grave' or 'Bowles' Variety' or interplanted with dwarf blue forget-me-nots.

Less reliably free to flower at an early age are the dwarf blue hybrids of R. *augustinii*. The most reliable of these and one of the slowest in growth is R. 'Sapphire' which will remain small enough for window box use for many years, after which it will do well if given a permanent home in an open position in any garden with acid or neutral soil.

Also good are the free-blooming dwarfs of the Lapponicum series of rhododendrons, such as the deep blue R. *scintillans*, yellow *chryseum*, white *microleucum*, red-purple *lysolepis* and hare-bell blue *hippophaeoides* which may be used together with delight-ful effect. The earlier, February and March flowering, R. *praecox* is good as a small plant with its pinky lilac, butterfly flowers, but after four or five years it will become too large for window box use and will need transferring to a tub or to the open garden.

Evergreen azaleas may be used in assortment to give a plea-santly flowery effect. Among the early, May-flowering, Kurume group with small pretty flowers and neat little leaves, many good colour varieties can be found. One of the brightest and freest is 'Amoenum' in magenta purple. It has a variety 'Amoenum Coccineum' with bright red flowers. Also lovely are 'Hinomayo' in pink, crimson 'Hinodegiri', salmon-pink 'Gaeshi' and 'Aioi' in rose-lavender. The rose-pink 'Kirin' has pretty hose-in-hose duplex flowers.

Rather later and slightly larger in flower are such hybrids as the rose-red 'Eddy', rose-pink 'Jeanette', 'Orange Beauty' and 'Pink Treasure'. These, however, need a shady box as they are apt to fade in strong sunlight and would soon present a streaky, dismal effect.

Less likely to fade but nevertheless appreciative of shade is the June-flowering, double, salmon-pink 'Balsaminaeflora' with its low, mounded habit and prettily rosetted flowers. This is lovely in association with the gentian-blue *Lithospermum* 'Heavenly Blue' or 'Grace Ward' which can be planted to trail over the front of the box. These would also be pretty if interplanted with the May-flowering dwarf broom *Cytisus kewensis* which makes foot-high cascades of sulphur moonlight each year without fail.

Lime-free soil is essential for rhododendrons and azaleas (also for the lithospermum mentioned) which in window boxes or tubs do best in the Royal Horticultural Society's camellia compost mentioned in the previous chapter.

Less expensive and very showy fillers for spring window boxes are to be found among the biennials. Double Brompton stocks and East Lothian stocks are excellent. Very early to flower, they last for a long time in bloom and are hardy and easy to grow. Delightful colour combinations can be built up, too. Favourites of mine are the rose-pink and lavender varieties planted together. I have used in conjunction also, lavender and purple and white varieties with good effect.

Window box owners with garden frames or greenhouses may like to grow their own plants from seed. They can be raised on sunny indoor window sills while mini-propagating units can be very useful. This will be discussed more fully in Chapter Nine.

If the Hansen strains of Brompton stocks are sown, it is possible to select only the double-flowered plants for growing on, as double and single forms have foliage in different shades of green. For the difference in the leaves to be pronounced the temperature has to be below 10°C (50°F), so it is necessary to sow the seeds in June and grow on the whole lot until October when the single-flowered plants can be differentiated easily and so discarded. Late October, when the summer occupants are past their best, is a convenient time to plant the stocks in the window boxes ready to flower the following spring.

Both Brompton stocks and wallflowers should be moved from their seed boxes to nursery rows and transplanted again in order to induce bushiness before they are ready to fulfil their final destiny in furnishing the window boxes.

Aspect is important. Stocks and wallflowers need a sunny position if they are to flower freely. Forget-me-nots will flower in shade as will polyanthus primulas—one of the best choices of all for window boxes on the north side of the house. Forget-me-nots with blue and sulphur polyanthus interplanted with the small ivory daffodil 'Mrs W. P. Milner' or the pale perianthed 'Rosy Trumpet' with pink and blue polyanthus would be pretty combinations for shady window boxes.

Wallflowers and forget-me-nots, unfortunately, do not do well in large cities. Atmospheric pollution upsets them so that they suffer if the winter is severe.

In smaller towns and in the country, however, a combination of forget-me-nots with pale sulphur, blood red or flame wall flowers is delightful, and the scent through the open windows above the boxes will amplify the pleasure.

The dark foliage of periwinkles makes a lovely background for bulbs and the double blue and wine-coloured rosettes of *Vinca minor* 'Azurea Flore Pleno' and 'Rubra Plena' give a delightful starry effect amidst white or pink Roman or Cynthella hyacinths and dwarf *Narcissus triandrus albus*—the Angel's-tears daffodil with its fly-away perianthed silver bells. This combination would do well even in a north-facing box as all the plants are shade tolerant.

Needing sun to open their creamy stars are the hybrids of

Tulipa kaufmanniana, the water-lily tulip. The paler ones such as 'Robert Schumann' (which does not have too red a stripe on the outside of the petals to detract from the creamy-primrose of their main colouring) associate with blue scillas, chionodoxas and muscari to make a delightful window box planting.

Some of the other tulip species and their hybrids such as the scarlet *T. eichleri* and orange-scarlet *greigii* are showy for window box use. These red-flowered species also look well with the small, blue-flowered scillas and muscari or they would form a rich contrast with sulphur or golden polyanthus. The larger-flowered species type tulips such as *T. fosteriana* 'Mme Lefebre' too easily catch the wind, however, and so are unsuitable in the rôle.

Double daisies (*Bellis perennis*) make a pretty interplanting for double early tulips as do early-flowering pansies and violas which for spring flowering should be sown the previous June. Small boxes filled with a combination of sulphur and lavender violas are very beautiful.

Chapter Four

Summer Colour

Geraniums, as they are commonly known—although the bedding plants we think of as 'geraniums' are truly pelargoniums—are not only among the most useful but also the most attractive plants for summer window box display. The tall zonals, in their many varieties, make fine upstanding plants and look well associated with lobelia or ageratum but dearer to my heart and, I think, better for the purpose, are the ivy-leafed forms with their semi-trailing growth.

As always, colour schemes must be chosen for their ability to associate with the background colour as well as that of the boxes. One of the prettiest schemes against a grey stone, cream or white washed wall is the warm pink 'Galilee' interplanted with lavender 'La France' or 'Mrs Martin'. Good against similar backgrounds would be a planting solely of the pale pink 'Mme Crousse'—or one might use this ivy-leafed variety in conjunction with a zonal of similar colouring such as 'Salmon Paul Crampel'. One might also intermingle 'La France' and 'Galilee' with the crisply pretty 'L'Elegante' with its single white, maroon-tipped flowers and cream-edged, rose-tinged leaves.

Red cultivars, also, are striking against a white or stone-coloured background, particularly when planted in black or black-and-white boxes. I like, also, to see several colours—purple, magenta, cherry, pink and lilac—planted in glorious medley with the softening influence of white to blend and unite the scheme. Red brick backgrounds are more difficult to suit. Here white geraniums associated with blue ageratum would be effective.

For deeper boxes on balconies, sun decks or stoeps, the lovely regal pelargoniums are superb with their luxuriant foliage and elegantly blotched flowers. In Britain however, they are suitable only for the milder areas on account of weather damage. In the south and east of Britain where sunshine hours are longer and the sun stronger the short-jointed 'Irene' zonals are good. These are among the most successful, too, in the States and on the Continent. 'Geraniums' as a rule prefer the sun, but I have grown them successfully in boxes facing north-east which got direct sunlight for only a couple of morning hours.

They may be planted directly into the boxes or set in individual pots packed into place with peat. They are best raised afresh for each season (see Chapter Nine for the method) from cuttings taken in mid-summer and wintered under glass.

Begonias, unlike pelargoniums, do best in shade and I have grown them in north-facing situations with success. A peat-sand compost or John Innes No. 3 suits them best. The large, camellia-flowered tuberous begonias in copper, salmon, blood-red and gold look well mixed, while the small-flowered *B. semperflorens* bedding varieties look best in single colour plantings. Striking varieties are 'Crimson Bedder' with reddish foliage and bright crimson flowers, and 'Fairy Queen' with dark green foliage and rose-pink flowers.

For large buildings, in-scale plantings are required to obtain a good effect. This necessitates the use of larger subjects such as evergreen azaleas in spring and dwarf-growing hydrangeas (such as the crimson 'Vulcan') in summer with shrubs like the berried pernettyas, clipped box or dwarf conifers for the winter months.

Hydrangeas need plenty of moisture. Their boxes should be as deep as possible and lined with rotted turf or black polythene (provided with drainage holes) to prevent drying out. Or they can be set into the boxes in individual pots which may afterwards be sunk in the ground in a sheltered place to winter outdoors. The R.H.S. camellia compost (see Chapter Two) suits hydrangeas well, or they can be grown in Levington compost where mixing facilities do not exist. Apart from the 12-inch 'Vulcan' (see the foregoing) young plants, two or three years from cuttings, give the best results. If ordering hydrangeas from a nursery for window box use, stipulate that they should supply *budded* plants. Alternatively hydrangeas purchased from a flower shop, although more expensive, will prove suitable for window box use.

Fuchsias are attractive and colourful subjects and there are certain semi-prostrate varieties with just the right habit for container cultivation. The pink and purple 'Rose of Castile', and cherry-red 'Marinka', rose and violet 'Margaret', creamy pink and mauve 'Lena' and pink and blue 'Alice Hofman' are some of those that can be relied on to cascade attractively over the edge of the boxes without growing too tall and so catching the wind. Many nurseries and garden shops offer a wide choice, making it easy to select varieties to complement the colour scheme of your dwelling. Where frost-proof shelter is available fuchsias may be overwintered and brought into bloom again the following season.

Fuchsias do well in John Innes No. 3 or Fisons Plantgrow with additional bonemeal. They are hearty feeders and benefit from regular liquid feeds and frequent watering to keep up their flower production. They will succeed in sun or shade—though they prefer dappled shade—but their heavy swing of flowers makes them unsuitable for windy sites.

Planted in individual pots that are packed into the boxes with peat they can readily be removed for overwintering in a frost-free shed, garage or cellar. They should be kept fairly dry through the winter. In early spring they should be cut back hard and moved into the warmth and the light. Repotting or topdressing with fresh compost as they begin to grow again will prove beneficial.

Heliotrope is an old garden favourite on account of its scent. It is useful, too, in that it will flower well in sun or shade. A box, composed solely of heliotrope, however, might look somewhat sombre but the purple flowers would look lovely in association with pink or flame antirrhinums or pink and purple fuchsias such as 'Lena' or 'Rose of Castile'.

A half-hardy, shrubby perennial, heliotrope can best be worked

42

in conjunction with a greenhouse or sun-porch from which frost can be excluded. Cuttings taken in spring can then be grown on to provide young, vigorous plants ready to bloom the same summer. Where no greenhouse is available, seed can be sown in a mini-propagator early in the year and the young plants brought on in a sunny window or heated sun-room ready to plant out in June. 'Princess Marina', 'President Garfield' and 'Gatton Park' are all good strains to sow.

For sunny window boxes there is a wide choice of biennials and annuals that can be bought quite cheaply from almost any nursery garden store in May and planted to flower from June on. It is important not to buy the plants too soon. In many areas, bedding plants appear for sale in the chain stores, outside the green-grocers and in the markets as early as April. Often these are not properly hardened off and if planted out before frost danger is past can produce only disappointing results. Lobelia, white and mauve alyssum, misty blue ageratum and dwarf golden tagetes are all available to fill shallow boxes or to use as edgings to front the display with taller 'geraniums', antirrhinums, and so on, at the back. *Phlox drummondii* with its pretty trusses of white, lilac, pink, purple and red is also good.

Petunias are lovely subjects for window boxes, but they need full sun if the flowers are to open freely. They are well able to withstand hot soil conditions at the roots. For sheltered boxes some of the large-flowered, ruffled hybrids are delightful. Of these I like the white 'Snowcap' and 'Cream Perfection' which are pretty in association with soft blue and mauve varieties such as 'Blue Lilac', 'Capri', and 'Blue Bell' or with pinks such as 'Pink Satin' and 'Pink Sensation'. I do not care for the striped sorts. The dark red 'Gipsy Ballerina' is effective, and the 'Cascade' varieties offer a good assortment in pink, red and white and are early in bloom with extra-large flowers. Their attractive waterfall habit of growth makes them suitable, also, to fill hanging baskets.

Plants may be bought readily but those who want to try the special strains would do well to raise their own, sowing in boxes indoors in February or March. The seeds germinate readily if covered with a sheet of glass or in a mini-propagator. It is important, however, to ensure that they are properly hardened off before transferring them to the window boxes in early May.

Sweetpeas do not often come to mind in connection with window boxes, but the 'Little Sweetheart' strain are particularly suitable with masses of frilly, sweetly-scented flowers. The plants are very compact in growth. They do well in city gardens but need a constant supply of moisture. Levington compost suits them well, and it is helpful to use a black polythene mulch to prevent the boxes from drying out. They can be relied on to do well even in a cool wet summer and so are particularly useful for British window boxes. The polythene mulch also ensures their success in Cape Town, Auckland or Californian gardens.

Antirrhinums are always useful and pleasing colour combinations may be built up. Lemon antirrhinums are good with soft blue ageratum. Pink antirrhinums and 'Blue Bedder' petunias look well, and I have used the soft flame 'Wisley Glow' with a deep purple petunia with striking effect. Again one's choice will depend on the colour scheme of the house. The soft orange and purple are attractive with yellow ham stone or with honey or mouse-coloured Cotswold stone.

Marigolds, whether of the small tagetes (French marigold) or large-quilled calendula (Pot marigold) type are good window box subjects. There is a dwarf double African marigold, 'Spun Gold,' which grows only 9 inches high and is useful. They look particularly effective in black boxes against white or cream walls, in hardwood boxes of polished teak or in cedar wood containers where the gleam of royal blue lobelia among their sunny orange and gold can be pleasing.

In warm countries with hot, dry summers and for boxes facing direct sunlight where their flowers can be relied on to stay open, the various mesembryanthemum species are useful to resist drought conditions. Lampranthus species in pink and purple are particularly attractive to drape the fronts of the boxes while the taller venidiums and arctotis will give more height.

Easily grown annuals that may be sown *in situ* to take over from spring-flowering polyanthus or violas are the bright blue-flowered dwarf convolvulus such as 'Royal Ensign'. These are lovely

44

interspersed with ruffled pale pink or white petunias, and will flower for a long period if conscientiously dead-headed, as is essential with all window box subjects if they are to give a lengthy display.

Some alpines such as *Campanula portenschlagiana*, which are so strong growing that they might sometimes be regarded as a nuisance in the rock garden, are delightful used in window boxes to blend in with larger flowers. The harebell-blue campanulas look well with pink antirrhinums or pelargoniums, while the white *C. isophylla* 'Alba', usually regarded as an indoor pot plant, is quite satisfactory for outdoor use in summer. Its white stars associate happily with pink or blue hydrangeas, or it may be used with pink or salmon zonal pelargoniums to disguise their tall stems and to clothe the foreground by draping the front and sides of the boxes.

Campanula isophylla 'Alba' increases fast, and rooted pieces may usually be pulled away from the parent plant and grown on in their own pots until they are ready to take their places outdoors. Pieces of *C. portenschlagiana* may also be pulled away from their parents in the outdoor garden and, so long as they are kept moist, will readily root and make large clumps in the window boxes. After flowering, I return them to the garden to grow on through the winter and spring ready to serve again the following summer.

Dwarf hebes (veronica), especially *Hebe speciosa* and its hybrids and cultivars, are useful in mild areas as not only will they produce their pink and purple bottle-brush spikes through late summer and autumn but, being evergreen, the bushes will remain decorative through the winter and if interplanted with bulbs will serve to clothe the boxes until summer comes round again. If interset with seeds of the dwarf blue convolvulus or Virginian stock they may be used as permanent furnishings, remaining in the boxes until they become too big. They strike readily from cuttings (Chapter Nine) so against this day one can always have young plants coming on.

Chapter Five

Autumn Brightness

Using interchangeable plastic liners or individual pots in the window boxes enables one to change the display as often as necessary. When the spring bulbs or wallflowers go over, one removes their complete liner and replaces it with another containing china asters, fuchsias, pelargoniums or petunias. Some of these subjects may well go on until autumn or one may have in readiness further liners holding dwarf chrysanthemums or Coltness dahlias starting to bloom.

Alternatively, by careful planning one box can be planted to supply both summer and autumn colour.

Nemesia, interplanted with dwarf Collarette dahlias or with Coltness Gem types, will give continuous colour from June until frost.

The nemesia should be dot planted, between and to the front of the dahlias. Flowering first, it can then be removed as its blooms fade, giving the dahlias full room to bush out.

All too often, in Britain, nemesias are seen as spindly, too delicate looking plants that never attain their full glory. This is because they are usually raised from spring sowings. Where it is possible to sow one's own and overwinter them under cool glass it will be found that a September sowing will yield much sturdier, more brilliant plants.

Coming from the mountains of Cape Province in South Africa,

they appreciate moist winter conditions that are cool and at the same time frost free. Sown in 3-inch pots they should be thinned out to one plant per pot and potted on when necessary into 6 inch pots. With a night temperature above freezing but below 4 °C (40 °F) they will become large, showy plants, ready to harden off and plant in the boxes in May when they will soon come into flower. Then, provided the dead heads are removed systematically, they will bloom for a long time, until the interplanted dahlias spread and begin to flower freely enough to take over the display.

Single or double Coltness Gem dahlias in mixed colours will give a seasonally cheerful harvest festival show. They are easily raised from seed either in a mini-propagator or on a sunny window-sill, or can be started under glass in February or March from tubers saved from the previous year.

If grown in liners they may be over-wintered by cutting off the blackened foliage after the first hard frost, leaving the tubers *in situ* and taking the liner indoors, either to the protection of a garage or shed, or to an unheated room or house-loft. They must be wintered cold but not allowed to become frosted. To this end the peat in which they are growing should be allowed to dry out. Indoors this peat will be sufficient protection, but if they are wintering in a garden shed, it may be as well to stack the liners together, covering them all with sacking or layers of newspaper to exclude the frost. Leaving the dahlia tubers in the peat prevents their loss from shrivelling or mildew.

To start them into growth the following season they should be brought into the light. Place them either in the cold frame, on the greenhouse staging or in sunny windows and water the peat well to activate them.

If started out of doors, they should be stood in a sunny, sheltered position and covered with sheets of glass. The glass should be lifted an inch or two during the day to allow the air to circulate. It should be lowered at night and sacking or thick newspapers placed on top to keep out the frost. When the dahlias are growing strongly, the glass should be left off but they will need to be brought under cover at night when frost threatens.

If they are to be interplanted with nemesia, they can be raised in individual pots which can be placed alternately in the window boxes and packed round with peat to keep them in position and to prevent drying out.

Among berried subjects, pernettyas stand out as being the most satisfactorily showy and also the easiest to manage in window boxes. Making dwarf evergreen bushes of a foot to 18 inches in height, they bear pleasant but not particularly conspicuous white heath flowers in spring, followed in autumn by berries as large as marbles, pink, red, lilac, purple or glistening white. The self-fertile 'Davies' Hybrids, by colour or in assortment, are the plants to choose.

Those with gardens will find them easy to manage in pots—sunk to the rim in the ground during the spring and summer—to be raised and transferred, still in their pots, to the boxes when their berries are enlarged, to replace the summer occupants as soon as these are past their best.

Dwarf chrysanthemums of the Otley strain make compact, colourful bushes. The smaller-growing of the Pompons such as 'Janté Wells' (yellow) are also useful and can be relied on to bloom for a couple of months in the autumn. They are ideally grown in pots like the pernettyas and used to replace summer-blooming subjects while at the peak of their own display. Alternatively they may be grown in liners.

The florists' specially-dwarfed pot chrysanthemums are attractive subjects for window boxes, although somewhat costly to buy in quantity. They will not retain their dwarf habit for a second season, unfortunately, but may be planted in the garden to provide cut flowers.

The use of liners makes it possible to change the displays fairly frequently so long as one has a garden or even a paved yard where the containers can stand while their inmates are brought into flower. Under these conditions, dwarf Michaelmas daisies such as the lavender 'Little Blue Boy' and rosy 'Little Pink Lady' are worth their turn.

Colchicums—those autumn-flowering bulbs that look like large crocuses—are good to use in conjunction with the dwarf Michaelmas daisies or with dwarf chrysanthemums or pernettyas.

The lilac hybrid 'The Giant', and species such as *C. byzantinum*, *speciosum*, its white variety *album* and its early-flowering variety *bornmuelleri*, can be relied on to produce clusters of up to 20 or more long-stemmed, large chalices from single bulbs. Interplanted, towards the front of the boxes, they provide focal interest and also lengthen the display, coming into flower before the pernettyas or chrysanthemums reach their peak.

Hebes, too, are good subjects for autumn and one of the very best is the purple-flowered 'Violet Queen' which has pretty dark green crinkly leaves backed with reddish brown. Its distinctive foliage and dark chocolate-red stems are almost as attractive as its elegant flower spikes. It is delightful in grey, white, yellow or light blue window boxes and can be left as a winter furnishing when it will often delight one by producing its bottle-brush flowers during mild spells. A tuft or two of winter jasmine, *Jasminum nudiflorum*, that has been well pruned back in early spring may be interplanted and its yellow stars will provide a charming colour combination with the purple flower spikes of the hebe, starting to bloom in late October in a sunny window box and flowering through until the spring.

Training winter jasmine in this way is an easy matter for those who have an established plant on a garden wall. As many gardeners know, the jasmine sends out roots to layer itself wherever its trailing branches touch the ground. These rooted shoots should be severed and individually potted up in autumn to be cut back the following spring. The next autumn they will yield a fair show of flowers and thereafter should be stool-pruned each spring to encourage bushy growth. For window box use all shoots should be stopped at 18 inches from the base. This will ensure the production of side shoots and thick showers of its sunny autumn and winter flowers.

Chapter Six

Winter Schemes

To take in the window boxes for the winter or to leave them empty is a pity because this is the time of the year when a little colour and eye-comfort is most to be appreciated. The house will look better and more furnished from the outside even if the window boxes are occupied solely by the greenery of wallflower plants or Brompton stocks overwintering ready for spring bedding. By using liners, however, one can do better than this. The wallflowers or Brompton stocks with their accompanying bulbs can spend the winter against the wall of the yard or patio, functioning as troughs on the terrace or sunk to their rims in a garden bed while replacement liners occupy the boxes, filled with subjects that can be relied on to bring winter brightness to the exterior of the house, thus extending to outdoors the welcome that awaits within.

Winter-flowering heaths, including the well-known *Erica carnea* cultivars, provide some of the best fillers for winter window boxes. Attractive both in and out of flower, with their hummocky shapes and fresh green or warm bronze foliage, they are ideal furnishing for the dullest months of the year.

The *Erica carnea* heaths are low growing and ideal for shallow boxes adorning small dwellings. For larger houses, office blocks and flats, the taller *E. mediterranea* 'W. T. Rackliff' with its moss-green foliage and white bells would be more in scale. This heath does not, however, come into bloom until February so—to provide a longer season of colour—the pinky rose hybrid *E. x darleyensis* 'A. T. Johnson', which comes into flower in December, would be ideal.

Good cultivars of the low-growing *E. carnea* are 'Winter Beauty', which opens its rosy bells from mid-December on, and the January–February blooming white-flowered 'Springwood' and the strawberry-ice 'Springwood Pink'.

The new 'December Red' is useful to give earlier colour. A 3-foot-long box planted with two of this cultivar flanked at each end by plants of 'Springwood Pink' would be effective over a full three-month period.

It is most important when ordering heaths for window boxes to make clear to the nursery that you want sizeable plants for immediate decorative effect. Small plants would be cheaper but would not make much of a show until the second year. I prefer to plant the heaths in the liners or in individual pots rather than directly into the boxes, so as to obviate the need for disturbance.

Beware of buying the showy Cape heaths that one sees in the flower shops to decorate British window boxes. Although these make wonderful window box displays in those areas of South Africa, New Zealand, Australia and the southern United States which do not experience severe frost, they would be killed very quickly by the rigours of the climate in winter Britain anywhere, except perhaps in the Scillies or Channel Islands.

Variegated euonymus is the slow-growing *E. radicans* 'Silver Queen', which may be bought as young plants and will grow quickly into bushes a foot or 18 inches tall at which height they may be kept, being sheared over each August after they have made their bushy growth. Silvery-white and fresh green in effect, plants of this cultivar may be pot grown ready to interplant in the window boxes with such ericas as 'Springwood' or 'Winter Beauty'. In black or light green boxes this euonymus is particularly effective with the white-flowered variety of heath.

Variegated periwinkles and ivies also are attractive and give interest to window boxes in winter. They may be pot grown or planted direct into the boxes or liners and allowed to trail over

the front, thus heightening the effect. Clipped back after flowering, even the vigorous *Vinca major* forms will remain compact
while at the same time being large enough in leaf and flower to
make a considerable show.

Early bulbs are delightful piercing through this evergreen
cover. Among them are snowdrops, of which the large flowered
Galanthus elwesii and the old-fashioned doubles do well in sunny
boxes, while the ordinary wildling prefers the shade. Very early
to flower, too, are some of the dwarf crocus species. *Crocus
ancyrensis*, often sold as 'Golden Bunch', and the lilac and fawn
sieberi will often flower by the end of January, while in February
the amethyst *C. tomasinianus*, and *chrysanthus* in its many forms,
will burst into bloom. Of *C. tomasinianus* the form known as
'Whitewell Purple' is perhaps the most satisfactory for window
boxes, being slightly larger and more sturdy and having chalices
of a lively purple that are bright on the outside of the petals as
well as within, and so are showy even on a dull day when no sunshine exists to expand the cups and reveal the bright orange of
the stigma and style.

The daffodil-yellow little *Iris danfordiae* is also very early to
flower and although it usually splits into small bulbs, and so is
unlikely to bloom a second year, it is cheap enough to be regarded
as expendable, so one can enjoy its cheerful splashes of sunshine
without feeling that one is being too extravagant.

An everlasting with a silvery effect to combine well with
Euonymus radicans 'Silver Queen' is *Anaphalis triplinervis* with
attractive close sprays of small, silvery-white daisies above its
silver-grey leaves.

Bergenias in general make rather large clumps of heavy but
beautiful foliage. With their glossy ribbed leaves and substantial
sprays of pink or rose-purple bells they are satisfying winter subjects for large window boxes. *B.* × 'Smithii' has smaller, spoon-
shaped leaves and solid spikes of warm pink flowers very freely
borne in mild spells throughout the winter.

For formal plantings, in the window boxes of Georgian or
Regency town-houses, or others of classical dignity, clipped box
plants or dwarf conifers are sometimes used. These serve the

purpose in providing winter furnishings but, where they are used, I think one should plant crocuses to add touches of bright colour in late winter and earliest spring.

Conifers, when chosen for the purpose, must be really dwarf. The upright-growing blue-grey Noah's Ark Juniper—*Juniperus communis* 'Compressa', is one of the most suitable, while *Chamaecyparis obtusa* cultivars make neat, chunky little bushes with rich green foliage in close-packed, fan-shaped branches. *C. pisifera* 'Nana' and *C. p.* 'Plumosa Compressa' offer several interesting golden and variegated forms.

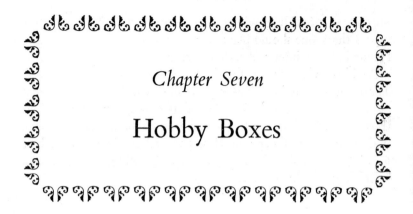

Chapter Seven

Hobby Boxes

Although it is desirable that the window boxes at the front of the house should be similar to each other in design and planting to confer the maximum decorative effect there is no reason why boxes to the rear or side windows need follow the same design. This gives opportunities to indulge in specialised plantings and hobby boxes.

Keen cooks living in flats or houses without kitchen gardens may enjoy raising their own herbs in window boxes beneath kitchen or bathroom windows. As with many other subjects, the most satisfactory method is to grow the herbs in individual pots sunk into the boxes. With herbs this is particularly important as it prevents the roots of extra-invasive subjects such as mint swamping and taking over the box to the exclusion of the others.

Of the commoner herbs, apple mint, *Mentha rotundifolia*; thyme, *Thymus vulgaris*, and the lemon-flavoured *Thymus citriodora* are excellent. Useful too are marjoram, *Origanum majorana*, French tarragon, *Artemisia dracunculus*; chives, and sage. Basil, too, is worth growing and there should always be a pot of the universally useful parsley.

Plants should be bought of the apple mint (which with its round, flannelly leaves makes the *very* best sauce), tarragon and chives. The rest are easily raised from seed.

Herbs are sometimes slow to germinate but boiling water

poured over the surface of the soil before sowing usually warms it enough to give the necessary impetus to start the seeds into growth.

Salading such as radishes and spring onions may easily be raised in window boxes and, although there will not be room for many lettuces, it is fun to grow one's own. The small, very sweet 'Tom Thumb' variety is one of the best lettuces for the purpose.

Whereas most herbs thrive in a sunny window box, salad vegetables are better in partial shade and if only a southern-facing window box is available it would be worth making a mini-awning from cardboard or canvas stretched over wire hoops to create shade during the hottest part of the day. Gaily painted with stripes this can add to, rather than detract from, the charm of the window box appearance.

Lettuce and radishes need a moisture-retentive compost such as John Innes No. 2, to which extra peat has been added, and must never be allowed to suffer from drought, otherwise the radishes become hard and woody, and the lettuces may bolt. You cannot get tender, juicy leaves if the roots are dry.

Radishes, in particular, are very quick to grow, taking only about three to four weeks from sowing to yield succulent roots for eating.

A first sowing of spring onions can be made in April, a second in May and a third about August. 'White Lisbon' is still one of the best varieties to pull in the young stage.

Lettuce may be grown from seed sown directly into the boxes or liners and thinned out as required or you may buy a dozen or so plants from your local nursery or plant stall, and dot-plant them in the boxes, cutting the middle plants first and leaving room for the others to grow on to a bigger size. Lettuces benefit from a light dressing of general fertiliser, a little dried blood or a liquid feed of Sangral every ten days. Half an ounce of dried blood or fertiliser is enough for one window-boxful of lettuces.

Alpine strawberries are not only pleasant to eat but decorative in growth. They will grow in any peaty compost if well fed, but plenty of moisture and fertiliser is essential as they are heavy feeders. Well-rotted manure, if available, incorporated into the compost will give them an extra boost. 'Baron Solemacher' is one of the best flavoured and is easily grown from seed.

The seeds should be sown in the autumn in John Innes No. 1. Cover the seed pans until the seeds have germinated, watering only sparingly. The small plants should be pricked out into individual pots or into window box liners to winter indoors in a sunny window or in a cold frame. They will even survive the cold on the balcony of a flat if the pots or liners are placed within a box for protection and covered with glass, which should be raised an inch or two during the day for ventilation, provided frost is not present. Put the young strawberry plants into the boxes in March, or April in cold areas, and they will bear fruit in the summer and on into the autumn.

Alpine strawberry plants quickly go past their best so a new batch should be raised every other year.

Miniature roses make interesting and appealing subjects for hobby boxes. They are usually sold in their own small pots which can be packed into the window box with peat or they may be removed from their containers and planted direct into the boxes in John Innes No. 3 compost. As the compost would need changing every two years, however, I think they are best kept in their individual pots and repotted into a larger size the following November.

Miniature roses occur in various colours and shapes. The best are in appearance tiny replicas of the popular hybrid teas. Dainty in growth they measure no more than 10–18 inches at maturity.

Miniature roses can be divided into two types: those with *Rosa roulettii* (syn. *R. chinensis minima*) parentage which grow to about 6 inches high and 6–8 inches wide with tiny fern-like foliage, and the mixed parentage hybrids, often descended from dwarf floribundas and hybrid teas crossed with dwarf china roses. These miniature hybrid tea and floribunda types grow later to 18 inches high and up to a foot across. These make the best window box subjects but the smaller-growing chinensis 'fairy' roses are suitable for stone sink or trough cultivation.

Good cultivars for window boxes are 'Baby Masquerade' (a miniature form of the multi-coloured floribunda), 'Josephine

Wheatcroft' (yellow), 'Scarlet Gem', 'Baby Gold Star', 'Coralin' (coral pink), 'Perle de Montserrat' (rose-pink), 'Posy' (deep pink) and 'Oakington Ruby'.

Unlike larger-growing roses, these dwarf kinds need very little pruning—just sufficient to keep a bushy, compact shape, apart from the removal of dead or damaged wood. Pruning can be done with a sharp knife or with nail-clippers, as the stems are very slender.

They may be increased by cuttings taken in late August and September and inserted into a peaty sandy compost or Levington seed and cutting compost and rooted in a cold frame. Where no frame is available they may be rooted in fibre pots, such as Jiffy pots or Root-o-Pots, stood in a wooden box kept close by a sheet of glass.

The cuttings should be about 3 inches long, taken with a heel and inserted into the pots on a slant. They should be wintered in a cold greenhouse or frame or on the window ledge of an un-heated room. In early April the pots should be stood out of doors on a base of sand or ashes in a sheltered spot. Light nipping back of the shoots at this stage ensures bushy plants to go into the window boxes in May or June. Should they be troubled with insect pests and mildew they should be lightly sprayed with malathion insecticide and dinocap or other reliable fungicide.

Cacti and succulents are interesting plants for hobby boxes in sunny positions. In many countries they may be left out of doors all the year round, but most are not hardy in Britain and so need to be taken indoors for the winter. To this end they are best planted in a liner which can be brought in and stood on a sunny indoor window ledge during the colder months while their place in the outside box is taken by 'Phoenix' wallflowers, Brompton stocks, alpines or periwinkle and mixed bulbs.

Contrary to what one might expect of such desert plants, John Innes No. 3 compost suits cacti well. During the growing period they should be fed occasionally with liquid fertiliser. Cacti grow very well also in Levington compost, without the addition of sand. The nutriment contained in the compost is sufficient for their needs, provided one tops it up during the growing season with an additional dressing of the same compost pricked in with a table fork. Correct watering is most important, making all the difference between failure and success. Cacti hibernate during the winter, and therefore should hardly be watered at all. In spring they should be sprinkled with water lightly, just to activate them, until they show signs of growth. Water is applied liberally only when the compost has dried right out.

During the growing period incipient buds show, the stems fill out and the crowns sprout new spines. Some cacti have a second dormant period in the summer when these signs of growth stop and water should be withheld until they start to grow again in late summer when they can be watered freely again until the end of September. After this, water should be decreased gradually and withheld almost altogether during the winter months, with the exception of grafted plants which need some water just to prevent the stock becoming too dry. An indoor winter temperature of 10 °C (50 °F) suits cacti best.

Both during the winter when they are living on an indoor window sill, and in the summer when they occupy the window box, cacti should have their containers turned regularly so that they do not become one-sided. During their growing period, particularly, they need fresh air and should go outside once the danger of frost is past. Choice will be governed by individual preference, but the various species of mammillaria, gymnocalycium and pseudolobivia will be found responsive and rewarding under hobby box conditions. Rebutia, too, is attractive, but needs colder winter conditions—just enough warmth to exclude frost being sufficient.

Alpines grown in window boxes can give a great deal of pleasure to the flat dweller or owner of a town-house without a garden. Whatever the aspect—whether in sun or shade—it will be sure to suit some of the delightful little wildlings from high mountainous regions in various parts of the world. For a sunny window box, John Innes No. 2 compost, with some leafmould added and additional grit and sand will make happy various treasures from the limestone Alps. In shade, the Royal Horticultural Society's camellia compost will suit the calcifuge shrublets that would normally find a home on a sandstone rock garden or in a peatery. Pieces of suitable rock should be two-thirds buried to give roothold and protection to the plants as well as to set off the boxes. Limestone rock may be used for the sunny box, but granite or sandstone would be safer for the lime-haters in the shady box.

Starting with tiny bulbs like the glorious blue *Iris histrioides* flowering alongside crimson- and white-flowered forms of *Cyclamen orbiculatum* in January, both boxes can be gay and interesting to the end of the year.

Most small bulbs suit either compost or aspect but when we come to the dwarf narcissi it is as well to remember that the shy-eared *Narcissus cyclamineus* with its long golden trumpets and fly-away perianth, prefers a moist, peaty compost in partial shade whereas the gay little hoop-petticoats of *Narcissus bulbocodium* will be happy in either box. The common dog's-tooth violet, *Erythronium dens-canis*, will be happy in the sunny box, but the choice North American *E. revolutum* or *E. johnsonii* do best in cool peat in shade. The spring gentian, *Gentiana excisa* (syn. *G. acaulis*) might be persuaded to yield its capricious flowers in sun. The autumn-blooming deep blue *G. sino-ornata* must have lime-free peat. The turquoise × *macaulayi* 'Well's Variety' is less fussy.

Saxifrages such as the early sulphur *elizabethae*, golden 'Haagii' and the shell-pink *irvingii* will combine with bulbs to make the sunny box gay in spring to be followed by small dianthus such as *freynii*, with its blue-grey leaves and rose-pink clove-scented flowers, and rose-red *neglectus* which is more compact than the British maiden pink, *Dianthus deltoides*. These may be followed by the smaller campanulas such as *C. arvatica* with its violet stars, white variety *alba* and *C. pulla* with its violet bells. The harebell-like *cochlearifolia*, pale blue *pilosa* and starry *garganica* are also non-rampant and suitable for these boxes in which rampant and invasive rock plants of the aubrieta and *C. poscharskyana* type are *personae non grata*.

Also suitable are the little androsaces, *Delphinium nudicaule* with its airily-spurred butterflies in red and chamois, crimson *Erinus* 'Dr Haenaele', summer-flowering easy *Gentiana cachemirica* and *gracilipes*, tiny geraniums such as the pale pink *argenteum* with its silvery foliage, the apple-blossom *dalmaticum* and beautifully veined pink *sanguineum lancastriense*, small penstemons such as the little lilac-flowered *menziesii* and crimson *rupicola*, tiny *Primula frondosa* (the bird's-eye primula) and the woolly leafed thyme— *Thymus pseudolanuginosus* (syn. *T. lanuginosus*).

In peaty composts in shade or partial shade one might try rare treasures such as the hepaticas of early spring, *Meconopsis quintuplinervia* (Farrer's harebell poppy), saintpaulia-like ramondas, and the beautiful shortias with their attractive leaves and pale-fringed flowers. Here might succeed the more choosy gentians such as the brilliant blue *G. angulosa* of spring, the lovely Cambridge-blue *farreri* and deep-toned autumn-flowering 'Kidbrooke Seedling', deep violet-blue *Cyananthus microphyllus* (syn. *C. integer*), haberleas, delicate little irises such as *cristata* and *lacustris*, the lavender-blue *Jeffersonia dubia*, beautiful lewisias, lithospermums, gay little mimulus such as *primuloides* and 'Whitecroft Scarlet', *Silene acaulis* and the double white *S. alpestris flore-pleno*, and the exquisite soldanellas.

Safe from slugs, many of these gems will thrive better in their boxes than under rock-garden conditions.

Favourite alpines which are too strong in growth for these hobby boxes may be used in the more formal window box displays in conjunction with bedding plants or bulbs. For this purpose would be suitable some of the mossy saxifrages, pretty alpine phloxes like 'Betty', 'Eva' and *douglasii* and the late summer-blooming bright blue *Ceratostigma plumbaginoides* with its reddish leaves.

Children enjoy growing plants in window boxes and it is ideal if they can be given a ground-floor box or patio trough in which they can plant and tend some of their favourites.

Most children enjoy growing bulbs for the spring, but September to March can seem a long time to the under-tens so it is a good idea to let them buy and plant in August a few autumn crocus corms or colchicum bulbs which will come into bloom within a couple of months and so make the waiting period seem shorter. For the same reason children should be given a few snowdrop bulbs and spring crocus corms to plant at the front of the box and cheer the days until the larger bulbs begin to flower.

Children enjoy growing pansies—they like the pretty cat-like 'faces'—so a clump of two of these scented charmers should be included in the children's box.

Seeds of Virginian stock will give a quick return from an April sowing. So will nasturtium seed sown later to give a succession. The large seeds of nasturtiums are useful, moreover, to teach a lesson in seed spacing and the velvety golden and flame trumpets and shapely green leaves are lovely to pick.

Some children will want to grow radishes or lettuce and in this, I think, they are to be encouraged. It matters little if a row of lobelia and alyssum at the front of the box is backed by the rosettes of a few lettuces, perhaps interspersed with a plant or two of pot marigolds or dwarf blue cornflower. The children are learning the secrets of plant growth and cultivation and they are enjoying the lesson. Moreover, gardening on a window box scale remains 'fun' and an important step in a child's development. It is the natural transition between a tray of mustard and cress flanked by a couple of saucers growing carrot top ferns on the inside window ledge and a bed in the outdoor garden which can to a young child seem endlessly weedy and disappointedly full of slugs and hard work. A window box of their own can help to instil in children the art of caring for plants and propagating their own without disappointment. It is in learning such delights young that true gardeners are made.

Chapter Eight

Routine and Problems

There is an art in managing window boxes that makes all the difference to their success. Few realise the thought and planning that lies behind the carefully manicured displays of hydrangeas and ivy-leafed pelargoniums that decorate the façades of some city buildings during the summer months, only to be replaced by the golden and tawny dwarfed chrysanthemums of autumn that are again succeeded by box or heaths for the winter to be supplanted by hyacinths and tulips in spring.

Flat dwellers and office gardeners find problems in the disposal of worn-out plants and soil and the transport of compost and plant food. They have to solve the difficulties presented by the fact that there is no one available for watering during holiday times and at weekends. Without facilities to mix their own composts and plant food they are dependent on easily available, clean and readily transportable products. For them, Levington compost, Plantgrow, Kerimure and the Bio seed and potting composts are the best answer. They can usually be bought in small bags that are not too heavy or bulky to take on bus or tube.

One can even carry them up the stairs if the lift is out of order. And where transport is available, of course, one can buy the larger sizes and so save time and labour. One must remember, however, that the plant foods in the compost will start to become

exhausted after six weeks or so. It is important, therefore, to feed
Liquinure every ten days after that period.

Drying-out at holiday times and weekends is likely to be a
problem, and it is a good idea to line the boxes (or plastic liners
if these are used) with several thicknesses of newspaper that have
been well soaked before being placed in position. One may also
cover the surface of the compost with black polythene (as described in Chapter Two), cut crosses in the polythene, fold it
back to form circles, and plant through these. The lining of wet
newspapers and the polythene soil-cover will help to reduce
evaporation, and should enable the boxes to be left after a heavy
soaking for up to a week even during a dry, sunny spell. Riviera
pots, with their built-in reservoirs of water, can be sunk into the
window boxes to supply another solution.

Drips from town window boxes can be an annoyance to
passers-by as well as a detraction from the appearance of the
building by forming trails of splashes and stains. To prevent this
nuisance it is important to have the window boxes fitted with
guttering as suggested in Chapter One, or else to use plastic
window box liners without drainage holes, adding charcoal
liberally through the compost so that it remains sweet and avoid-
ing over-watering which would cause waterlogging at the roots
and so kill the plants.

For flat dwellers the constant renewal of plants because of
lack of room to sink reserve containers into the soil and so econ-
omically to ring the changes means considerable expense. For this
reason cheaper plants may have to be chosen, such as early
'Phoenix' wallflowers, to clothe the boxes in winter and provide
spring flower colour, followed by petunias. Ivy-leafed and zonal
pelargoniums are expensive but can be increased by cuttings
(see Chapter Nine) rooted and wintered indoors, so from a
couple of geranium plants, combined with one of the cheaper
subjects such as ageratum or blue *Convolvulus minor* raised from
seed, it should be possible to raise enough geraniums to stock the
boxes the following season.

The use of plastic liners is a great convenience wherever room
can be found on a terrace or in the garden for the plants in the

spare containers to pass their off-season. This enables one more easily to ring the changes. Provided the composts are renewed by topdressing, some of the more permanent plants such as heaths and hydrangeas can spend up to three years in the same window box liner.

As the seasons change a container of winter-flowering heaths might be removed and sunk to the rim in the soil in a sheltered sunny spot, while their place in the window box is taken by another liner filled with hyacinths or early tulips combined with blue chionodoxas or polyanthus in a suitable colour. This in turn would be removed, the bulbs being planted out to decorate the garden for years to come and the polyanthus heeled-in in a shady spot to be divided if necessary, kept well watered, fed with bonemeal and brought on ready to go back into their container in the autumn.

Meanwhile, lining containers or individual pots of dwarf azaleas or rhododendrons would have gone into the window boxes to provide the early summer display, while the pelargoniums or petunias destined for use from mid-summer to autumn would have been planted in the liner from which the bulbs were removed and be growing on in a sheltered corner of the terrace or patio until needed.

When the summer bedding plants in their turn were done, they would have been replaced by the heaths, by berried pernettyas in individual pots, or by a display of variegated periwinkle and ivy interplanted with bulbs. It pays to plan ahead.

Care of the plants used in window boxes is all important. Heaths and periwinkles should be sheared back after flowering, as should aubrieta and alpine phlox. All flowering plants should be dead-headed daily if possible. This is important both from the point of view of appearance and also to encourage the production of flowers.

Tools for the window box gardener include a pair of scissors for dead-heading and cutting back, a pair of secateurs, a sharp knife for taking cuttings, a trowel (one of the narrow type sold for bulb planting is best), a large table fork to loosen the soil

1a. Ivy-leaved 'geraniums' make summer window box subjects *par excellence*.

1b. *Campanula isophylla* is useful to interplant between other material and can readily be increased from rooted pieces pulled off and wintered indoors.

2.   Pelargoniums add sophisticated colour to a London window box.

3a. Hanging baskets and containers give a flowery welcome to all who approach the front door of this modern bungalow.

3b. A tongued and grooved 'trough' window box gives deep root-hold and can be used beneath a low window to team up with an attractively planted basket suspended from the eaves of a single-storey dwelling.

4. Clematis like this can be grown in a tub and trained on a Netlon panel.

5a. Scheme for paved terrace with water-lily tank and decorative pots on coping.

5b. Well planted tubs and varied textures have been used to add interest to this paved area.

6. Suitably planted precast containers and wall baskets add focal colour where it is most needed in the design of this small garden.

7a. Crocuses to be followed by Dutch irises are beautifully in scale with this Victorian urn.

7b. Crocuses for early colour, followed by coloured primroses and auriculas for later bloom, are interspersed with aubrieta and *Cineraria* 'White Diamond' to set off their beauty in this flower-box built of reconstituted stone.

8a. Tubs of shrubs give a country air to this London roof garden.

8b. Wall shrubs and climbers may be planted in attractive pottery containers.

9. Oak tubs such as this offer permanent homes for hydrangeas or other shrubs.

10a. A Cotswold bird-bath planted with winter-flowering heather serves to brighten the Christmas scene, while the birds have luxury bathing facilities not far away.

10b. Pelargoniums and trailing lobelia are decorative in urns like this but would look better without the harshly contrasting spiky foliage.

11a. Reproduction stone troughs are among the wide variety of containers available today and have the advantage of being portable and easy to place. Filled with seasonal bedding plants in succession they can add colour to porch or patio throughout the year.

11b. A modern precast container is filled with cherry pink 'geraniums' and fluffy lavender-blue ageratum to distract the eye from an ugly inspection cover.

12. Pots of miniature roses and an alpine sink add interest to this planting of shrubs in tubs.

13. Daffodils are favourite subjects to fill containers for spring, and are also excellent for window box use.

14. Stone containers like this one make excellent focal features. Luckily, Verine reproductions of antique troughs and urns can be obtained at much less cost.

15a. A pleasantly planted decorative container filled with pelargoniums and impatiens.

15b. Tubs of pelargoniums have been used to mark the four corners of a formal pool in this large garden.

16a. This hundred-years-old wheelbarrow makes a unique container for an arrangement of pot plants at the doorway of a modern dwelling.

16b. Plastic containers like this may be sunk into the ground to provide colour at any chosen site, or they may be brought into bloom in a greenhouse ready to slip into a suitable container outdoors. Planted with successively blooming subjects, they can be used to supply containers throughout the year.

regularly to prevent caking, and a 1-gallon watering can with a fine-rose spray.

Wind can be a problem with window boxes at the seaside and in exposed places. Bushy, well-rooted plants resist wind best and most annuals and biennials such as wallflowers, antirrhinums and the various types of stocks benefit from pinching back in the early stages to encourage the production of side shoots. To prevent wind rock it helps to bury a stone to windward of the roots to anchor the plant on the side to which one can expect it to be blown.

Pinching back not only encourages the plants to put out side shoots and to make more roots, thus making them sturdier and better able to resist the wind, but also results in freer flowering.

Heavy overhead drip from the roof in wet weather may spoil the flowers. This will usually be prevented by adequate overhead guttering. Driving rain, too, can be a menace so it is as well to plant small, tough flowers of the French marigold, ageratum, sweet alyssum, lobelia and even the hydrangea category in weather-vulnerable situations and to reserve one's choicer subjects such as the double pelargoniums, tuberous-rooted begonias and ruffled F_1 hybrid petunias for a more sheltered box or patio trough.

Heavy drip and rain can lead also to soil caking. A polythene mulch can prevent this, alternatively after heavy rain one should tease the surface of the compost with a table fork to aerate the soil.

Cats and pigeons are sources of window box troubles. Where they are sufficiently active to constitute a menace I would suggest placing a grid of inch-mesh wire-netting over the box. Plants will grow happily through the mesh which will serve to hold them firm against wind rock.

Soot and air pollution clog the stomata on the leaves through which plants breathe. This seems to occur even in clean air zones, so it is helpful to syringe the foliage with a fine spray of tepid water at least once or twice a week to wash it clean. Where time permits a daily spraying, the plants will show their appreciation of this benefit with healthy foliage colour and increased vigour.

Pests and diseases do not on the whole cause a great deal of trouble to the window box gardener. Greenfly on miniature roses, petunias or lettuces is perhaps the worst problem, and this can be remedied easily by the use of insecticide dust in a puffer pack.

Botrytis or mildew is sometimes troublesome, the solution being to remove and burn affected leaves and buds and to dust the plants with flowers of sulphur or to spray with a suitable fungicide such as dinocap (a wettable powder which must be dissolved in water).

Sometimes seeds sown *in situ* may be subject to damping off, and it is a wise precaution against this trouble always to dust the surface of the soil or compost with flowers of sulphur.

Perennials and shrubs used in window boxes should be found sheltered places in the garden to pass their off-seasons. Some, like the polyanthus and periwinkles, may be set directly into the soil and kept well watered until re-established. Others, like the azaleas and hydrangeas, should be kept in the pots sunk into the ground to their rims against drying out.

Most bulbs need a year or two in the garden borders to build themselves up before serving another turn in the window boxes. Tuberous begonias and dahlias should be dried off in their pots or containers and overwintered indoors or in a frost-free place. Alpine plants and bulbs may remain in their containers for several years, provided they are topdressed annually with suitable compost (see Chapter Seven).

Chapter Nine

Raising your own Plants

Stocking one's window boxes can be expensive, so it is obviously a sensible proposition, where possible, to raise one's own plants. Not everyone, of course, has a greenhouse or cold frame, but one can do wonders on a well-lit indoor window ledge, while the addition of one of the reasonably priced mini-propagators such as the Humex Pottagator or Autogrow small propagator will soon pay for itself in the increased pleasure of growing things, and in the very real saving effected in the price of ready-grown plants.

Cuttings may be taken easily and conveniently from the zonal and ivy-leafed 'geraniums' and from the Regal pelargoniums. They should be about 2–3 inches long and consist of unflowered side shoots cut from the parent plant with a sharp knife at the end of July. The cutting should be cleanly severed, straight across, at a point just below the node or 'joint' (from which point the roots will later emerge), and the side leaves removed, leaving just the top 'tuft'. Oddly enough, the best results seem to be obtained if the cuttings are laid aside overnight and allowed to wilt before being inserted in Levington potting compost, John Innes No. 1 or a peat/sand or vermiculite mixture. It is worth potting the cuttings individually in 3-inch pots so that they can grow without disturbance until they are ready for potting on. Hydrangea cuttings respond to the same method.

All pots must be clean and crocked with a layer of stones or broken pot to cover the drainage holes.

It is important that all cuttings are firmly anchored in the compost and, to ensure this, it is necessary to see that the compost is firmly packed. I like to add the compost a little at a time, firming each layer down with the fingers.

A pencil may be used as a dibber to make the holes into which the cuttings will be inserted. A sprinkling of sand at the bottom of the hole helps the cuttings to root. The cuttings should be 'firmed' gently into place. Water well after the cuttings are inserted, and then allow them to become fairly dry until they start to root.

If a propagating case is available, it prevents excessive moisture loss and helps the leaves to plump up again. Alternatively, one can use a polythene bag, supported by three sticks inserted round the edge of the pot and secured by an elastic band around the rim. This forms a very 'close' and moist atmosphere, and is essential where trickier subjects such as fuchsias and heliotrope are to be rooted, but I have usually found that pelargoniums and hydrangeas root without difficulty. It is important that the shoots selected are not too hard. The softer the material in the case of cuttings of this type, the more readily it will root. Once the cuttings are firm and growth begins the polythene should gradually be left off or too-soft growth will result. It is best to leave off the polythene bag for a few hours at a time only at first, as if it is removed altogether too soon, the cuttings sometimes collapse.

Cuttings will start to root in two to three weeks. The ivy-leafed varieties with their thinner stems are more difficult to strike. With these, however, September cuttings will usually succeed.

Violas and pansies may be propagated from cuttings taken in September. Each cutting should consist of a healthy tufted side shoot 2 or 3 inches long, cut straight across below a node and inserted 3 inches apart in pans or trays of Levington compost or John Innes No. 1 and placed in a cold frame or wooden box covered with a sheet of glass and kept close until they start into growth, after which the glass covering should be raised a couple of inches in all but frosty weather. In prolonged frost the frame or box should be covered with sacking.

In spring the ventilation should be increased until finally the glass is left off altogether. The young plants may be set in the window boxes at the end of March or in April or May to fit in with the flowering sequence.

Heaths may be propagated from cuttings, but it takes a long time to build up plants large enough to create a window box display from cuttings, whereas established plants may be encouraged to layer by mounding the compost over the sides of the plants. This encourages the side shoots to root, and by this method it is often possible to remove sizeable portions of rooted plant from the parent and pot them on alone to build up into reasonably sized clumps for the following season.

The side shoots of pernettyas, too, usually form roots and, as with the heaths, it is usually quite easy to pull off rooted divisions that will fairly quickly build up into individual plants.

Seed sowing is the most economical way of raising new plants from seed. As with most garden operations, however, it is important to plan well ahead. Pansies, violas, double daisies and Brompton stocks intended for late spring window box display must be sown the preceding June. Similarly where greenhouse temperatures of over 10 °C (50 °F) will not be available in February, it pays to sow antirrhinums and annual chrysanthemums at the beginning of September, when the seeds will germinate easily without heat. Pricked out in October they can winter in a cold frame (or even in a box covered with a sheet of glass; the glass being raised an inch or so for ventilation purposes on all frost-free days). Early in April the plants should be transferred to 5-inch fibre pots and have their tops pinched out to encourage them to bush out ready to occupy the window boxes in May.

Dwarf 'Cupid' sweetpeas, too, may be autumn sown. In their case it pays to chip the seed cases before sowing, to facilitate germination.

Biennials such as wallflowers, sweet williams and forget-me-nots should be sown in the open ground at the end of May. Thinly sown in shallow drills, they quickly germinate. The wallflowers and sweet williams should be twice transplanted—once at the four-leaf stage and later when they have made 2–3 inches of growth. Plants left longer than this before the second transplanting will become spindly and apt to catch the wind when they take their places in the boxes for the following spring's display. Brompton stocks, too, although sown a month later, should go through the same process of twice transplanting.

Half-hardy annuals such as petunias, lobelia, ageratum, dwarf zinnias, French and African marigolds and China asters need to be sown in heat in February or March if they are to build up into sturdy plants to fill the window boxes in summer.

Levington seed compost or John Innes seed compost are among the most suitable for the purpose and both have the advantage that they may be bought from most garden shops and many ironmongers and multiple stores.

Seed should be sown in well-crocked pans, pots, seed boxes or plastic seed trays with drainage holes. When using boxes or trays, the crocks may be omitted but a good layer of fibrous roughage (rotted turf, bracken stalks or woody stems of the previous year's annuals, dried and saved) used to replace them.

Fill the containers with the compost, shake them to settle it down and then firm it into place with the bottom of a bottle or glass jar. Water it gently with a fine-rosed can before sowing.

The seeds should be sown thinly and evenly, and covered over with a light dusting of sieved soil. Large seeds such as dwarf sweet-peas or *Convolvulus minor* should be more deeply planted. Once the seeds are sown, the pots and pans should be covered with glass and brown paper or newspaper until germination takes place.

Provided the compost was moist before sowing, it should not be necessary to water until the seed leaves appear. Watering should be very gently done, using a can with a fine rose so as not to disturb the seedlings.

Before germination takes place, the covering glass should be lifted each morning and wiped free of condensation which might cause damping off. As soon as the soil greens over with the emergent shoots, both glass and paper should be discarded.

As soon as the seedlings are big enough to handle they should be pricked out individually, each into a composition pot such as a Jiffy pot or Root-o-Pot, into John Innes No. 1 compost. Make sure the compost is moist and, using a pencil as a dibber to make the planting holes, gently drop a seedling into each, afterwards firming the soil.

Potting the seedlings individually in this way enables them to be grown on into the kind of stocky, well-grown plants that are essential for window box display. Most window box subjects such as antirrhinums, *Phlox drummondii*, ageratum, heliotrope, impatiens and penstemons should have their growing tips pinched out at an early stage to encourage bushy growth.

It is important to see that all the plants are properly hardened off by being placed in an open frame or, if this is not possible, by standing them out of doors throughout most of the day and until they are ready finally to be left out at night in a sheltered place. After a week or ten days of this treatment they will be ready to take their places in the window box.

Polyanthus primulas may be raised from seed or increased by division of established plants when they are removed from the window boxes to be planted out in a reserve bed until they are needed again.

Choose a shady but not root-ridden site and incorporate some well-soaked peat with the soil before inserting the divisions.

As the plants are lifted, it will be seen that many of them have formed two or three crowns and rosettes of leaves. By holding the crowns firmly between the thumb and forefinger of either hand it will usually be possible to pull them apart. Occasionally, in the case of old plants with hard, woody crowns, it may be necessary to complete the division with a sharp knife.

Plant the divisions separately at least 4 inches apart and keep them well watered until established.

Tuberous-rooted begonias are spectacular window box plants and are very worth while as they will succeed well in shade where their large, brilliant blooms will last almost twice as long. It is cheaper to raise them from dry corms purchased from the garden shops or ironmongers in March rather than to buy flowering plants from the florist.

I like to plant the tubers in 5-inch pots which I can sink into the boxes and pack with peat. There is then no need to disturb the tubers when they are growing well. Levington compost or John Innes No. 3 suit begonias well.

Like hardy cyclamen it is sometimes a puzzle to tell which side of a begonia tuber is the top. This is usually hollow or flat, however, and has an area clear of wispy roots where the old stem grew. Keep this uppermost.

Crock each pot and half-fill the pot with compost. Sit the tuber on the compost and pack more compost in until the tuber is covered. Stand the pots on a light window sill in a cool or unheated room or put them in a sun-porch or cold frame. The compost should be moist but be careful not to over-water the pots until growth starts, otherwise the tubers may rot.

When the shoots appear, shade them from strong sunshine or the leaves may be scorched. Gradually harden them off by getting them used to outdoor conditions. Then as soon as frost danger is past the begonias can go out into the window boxes or tubs.

Small propagators are a great help in raising your own plants. The smallest can stand on a table near the window in the kitchen or living room of a flat and, even without heat, reproduce the close, moist conditions that enable cuttings to root and seedlings to germinate fast. If one has room, however, one of the larger, electrically heated types will be more worth while, enabling one to raise enough plants to stock several window boxes at a time. One of the simplest is the Autogrow propagator which takes four seed trays and has a sturdy polythene cover to ensure a close atmosphere. There are two models, one, thermostatically controlled, making it possible to retain any required soil temperature.

Humex Ltd also manufacture a reliable range of propagating equipment. For the flat dweller their Pottagator is a realistic investment, consisting of an electrically heated base with tray for seeds or cuttings and a clear, lightweight plastic cover to conserve moisture.

The Camplex seed propagator is another lightweight unit consisting of a deep plastic trough in which an electric heating cable is embedded in a layer of sand. An adjustable rod thermostat

controls the temperature and it is covered with a 10-inch-high polythene dome, giving adequate headroom for plants and cuttings.
Measuring about 2 by $2\frac{1}{2}$ feet, it is big enough to enable one to
raise several batches of seeds and cuttings at a time. Zinnias,
petunias, French and African marigolds, verbena and heliotrope
are easily raised in it, and fuchsias, pelargoniums and chrysanthemums are quickly rooted. For the ambitious window box gardener this is perhaps the best choice of all. The cable is rated at
75 watts, so it can run non-stop for over 13 hours on one unit of
electricity; controlled by a thermostat, as it is, it seldom operates
the whole time and is unlikely ever to use a whole unit in any
one day, so it is not expensive to run.

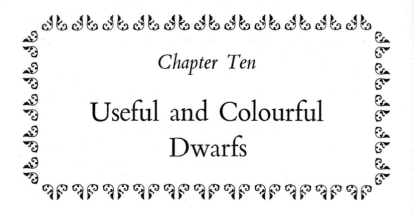

Chapter Ten

Useful and Colourful Dwarfs

Many plants that are attractive in form or colour and useful for their long season of flower or interest, are normally thought to be unsuitable for window box use because of their size. Compactness of growth is important above all things, when considering plants for window boxes, not only for appearance' sake, but also because of wind problems. However, some plants that one might otherwise dismiss from one's mind on account of their size, have dwarf, compact forms, making them eminently suitable for the job.

One such particularly attractive subject is *Campanula lactiflora* 'Pouffe' which has all the charm of the taller *lactiflora* varieties but bears its lavender-blue bells on foot-high mounds. Planted with pink *Geranium endressii* 'A. T. Johnson' it is useful where late summer/autumn subjects such as dwarf dahlias or China asters are to be used, because it will fill the gap, tiding over after the end of the spring display until the late-summer occupants come into bloom. This combination would be good also in a shallow trough or tub.

Dwarf white lavender is delightful to front taller-growing plants such as hydrangeas or zonal geraniums. It is not only uncommon but has a very long flowering season, coupled to the added bonus of scent and the possibility of harvesting its sweetly fragrant flowers to fill sachets to sweeten one's linen store, or to sell at charity Bring-and-Buys or Coffee Mornings. *Lavandula spica* 'Nana Alba' is the name to guide one's catalogue search.

Salvias of the perennial type always seem to have more charm than the militant scarlet kinds used for bedding. Very effective for use with white and pink petunias is the dwarf 'Lubeca' form of the deep blue *Salvia* × *superba*. The half-hardy *S. patens*, with its very attractive bright blue flowers, might be considered as an alternative to the scarlet salvias. Charming with silver-leafed *Senecio cineraria* and pink ivy-leafed pelargoniums, it is easily raised from seed in a mini-propagator.

For deep, balcony boxes and troughs, the dwarf *Thalictrum aquilegifolium* 'Purple Cloud' is useful and might associate with the small-growing *Gypsophila* 'Rosy Veil' to give a delightful misty background to the more often seen ageratum, heliotrope and pink candytuft combination.

Evergreen box is sometimes used for winter schemes and here again it is very important to get the right form. *Buxus sempervirens* 'Suffruticosa' is the edging box which retains its dwarf height, and readily clips into miniature pyramids or Noah's-ark trees for window box use. Also slow growing is the variegated *B. s.* 'Elegantissima' in which the dark green leaves are edged with yellow.

When raising annuals from seed it is necessary to be sure to choose a dwarf strain. Not all local sundriesmen and stores carry a complete range so it is as well to send for the catalogues of the leading firms such as Walter Blom, Sutton's, Dobie's, Bee's etc. (see lists), and browse through them carefully to pick out the strains which will yield compact, bushy plants of the type needed. Here again, some plants which might normally be thought too tall may well prove to have dwarf counterparts which will make ideal window box plants. Such are the 'Sweetheart' sweetpeas.

Russell lupins are plants that one would instantly dismiss when considering possibilities for window box or container display. Yet the dwarf 'Minarette' strain yields plants about 18 inches high that would be ideal for a balcony trough or deeper boxes. The colours are well mixed with, perhaps, a warm pink predominating.

African marigolds were, for many years, too tall for window boxes, but now there is a variety of dwarf strains which with their bushy growth, dense flowering habit and tough, weather-resistant blooms, are first rate. The chrysanthemum-flowered 'Spun Yellow' is one of the best with 3-inch wide, canary-yellow blooms on 12-inch plants. It is early and continuous in flower, and makes a good associate for companions in blue or lavender or with coppery French marigolds. Another compact African kind is 'Golden Age', with large, orange-gold double flowers. A good French marigold to associate with this or with 'Spun Yellow' is Dobie's early-blooming 'King Tut' with golden-centred, mahogany-red flowers.

Pot marigolds or calendulas are sometimes looked on as cinderella flowers, probably because they are so easily raised and so hardy and trouble free. In gardening, as in life, one is apt to put the highest value on the things for which one has struggled most. A fine compact strain that is good for windy areas, and has just the right habit for window boxes is 'Baby Orange', which grows to 12 or 15 inches high and has wide, double, tangerine-coloured flowers that combine well with lobelia.

Verbena is a compact plant for small window boxes or to plant towards the front of larger ones. It is useful, too, to mix with other plants in troughs and pots. Two good colours are to be found in the salmon-pink 'Compliment' and rose-purple 'Perfecta' strains. These go well together or in association with blue ageratum, 'Cambridge Blue' lobelia and lilac and pink ivy-leafed pelargoniums.

Some antirrhinums grow too tall for window boxes but the 'Wisley' strains can be relied on to produce compact flowers with the added essential that they are resistant to rust. The apricot-pink 'Juno' is good. The F_1 extra-vigorous dwarf 'Floral Carpet' type are fine for exposed places and result in a mixture of attractive colours and 8- to 9-inch mounded plants. A selection of these, called 'Floral Carpet Rose', is a good 'self' for colour-scheme planting.

Impatiens will succeed in sun or shade and an outdoor Dutch strain of F_1 hybrids gives good results in window boxes and containers, being very weather resistant and able to recover quickly, even after heavy dashing by rain. Known by the suffix 'Imp', 'Carmine Imp', 'Orange Imp', 'Rose Imp', 'Purple Imp', 'Scarlet Imp' and 'White Imp', all are useful. There is also a carefully blended scheme of colours in the 'Imp Formula' mixture. All these are well worth looking out for.

China asters are long lasting and have long been useful for late summer/autumn schemes. Hybridists have been working on earlier-flowering and wilt-resistant strains. These can be sown in liners or pots out of doors and transferred to the boxes when ready. Self-colours are available in some strains, and there are very dwarf forms 8- to 12-inch high which are specially suitable for windy situations.

Scarlet salvias, although sometimes rather blatant, can be first rate for formal schemes in town window boxes and two of the best, weather-resistant, compact dwarfs are 'Little Red Riding Hood' and 'Scarlet Pygmy'.

Ageratum is among the most popular and useful of all window box subjects. The usual pretty blue can be supplemented by 'Violet Cloud' and 'White Cushion' which are subtler and more fluffy than sweet alyssums of the same colouring.

PART TWO

Container Gardening

Colourful use of containers adds charm to this small garden

Chapter Eleven

Containers in the Garden Scheme

Tubs and pots, troughs and urns, built-up brick boxes, sinks, pensioned-off wheelbarrows, wrought-iron cauldrons and pottery jars—all have their part to play in the modern garden.

Whether used to contain rooting material in places where there is no soil—such as on balconies, stoeps, roof-gardens, backyards, patios, terraces—to provide emphasis marks on steps or paving or to stand on their own specially paved areas in the lawn, containers fill a strongly decorative rôle. In the first instance, however, utility may be the prime consideration.

On the tiny balcony of a city flat, high above the roofs of Cape Town, overlooking the London traffic or amid the concrete jungles of San Francisco or Sydney, the first need is to find something to hold enough soil to grow a few flowering plants to enliven the man-made surroundings, to give a sense of the luxury of outdoor living and to bring a glimpse of half-forgotten country gardens into town.

The containers must be light in weight and easily portable. They must be pleasing too—attractive in their own right yet not so striking as to detract from the plants they hold. Containers should complement and enhance the plants. If possible, also, they should fit in with the mood of their surroundings. Concrete and stone—even marble—Japanese and Italian pottery seem to go with modern high-rise buildings; wood, terra-cotta and wrought-iron suit the half-timbering of a country inn. Some of the elegant fibre glass reproductions of antique urns, tanks and jardinières in lead or stone finishes fit in with the restrained embellishments of a period house.

Containers must be in proportion to the plants. When dealing with large plants (standard rhododendrons, crape myrtle, topiary clipped box or yew, well-grown camellias, hibiscus or Portugal laurel), the container is of secondary importance and should be as plain as possible. Round or square wood tubs suit them best, according to the context of their surroundings.

In the case of such smaller yet still sizeable plants as young camellias, orange or lemon trees, oleander, yucca, agapanthus and *Phormium tenax* (New Zealand Flax), the pots have equal importance with the plants. Terra-cotta pots, olive-oil jars, reproduction designs and handsome square tubs have their place here.

Small flowering plants with little height suit either the reproduction troughs, tanks and urns, or shallow, concrete, circular tubs and low concrete bowls tapering from wide-diameter rims to narrow base. An overall flowery effect is to be aimed at with colourful sprays of ivy-leafed pelargoniums or strong-growing petunias tumbling over the firm rim of trough or bowl.

Unconventional containers such as retired wheelbarrows, painted in white, pale yellow or green can hold a gay assortment of bulbs or bedding plants to grace the sun-deck, verandah or stoep of a modern or traditional dwelling. A school tuck-box, painted white to contrast with its black iron bands—an old oak cradle—anything plain and well made may be pressed into service as a container for seasonal planting.

Casks are among the best of all containers. Sometimes they may be bought from a local brewery or one may obtain small vinegar barrels or large lard tubs from a wholesale grocery warehouse (all must, of course, be well scrubbed and thoroughly cleaned before use). Failing this, one can buy purpose-built barrels and casks from a coopery such as will be found among the suppliers listed at the end of the book. Cut in half, they make excellent containers for rhododendrons, camellias, hydrangeas, conifers, topiary shapes, oleanders, hibiscus, mimosa or small

gums (eucalyptus) (Fig. 7). For ease in moving, all wooden con·
tainers should be mounted on castors. This is particularly important when the tubs are destined to hold tender subjects which
might need to be taken into greenhouse or sun-porch for the
winter or moved to shelter during times of frost. Tubs and casks
should be charred before planting. This can be done by lighting a

*Half cask forming tub for
hydrangeas or other flowers*

FIGURE 7.

fire of shavings or paper inside and allowing it to burn until the
wood is charred to an eighth of an inch deep. To put the fire out,
simply turn the tub upside down on the ground.

Holed pots and casks, intended for strawberry cultivation, offer
attractive homes to ivy, trailing lobelia, ivy-leafed pelargoniums,
pendulous begonias, and so on.

83

Climbers—not only the ubiquitous sweetpeas but clematis, jasmine, morning glory (*Ipomoea hederacea*), *Solanum crispum* and *S. jasminoides* may be grown in casks and tubs if a 3-foot depth of plastic-mesh netting is placed to form a cylinder above the container; the mesh offering support to the climbing stems or tendrils. Green or white mesh may be used according to the type of container and background colour. The white mesh looks attractive with white painted tubs, of which the hoops have been picked out in black.

In areas with cold winters, of which Britain unfortunately is one, it may be more convenient to grow only completely hardy subjects in one's outdoor containers. But where winter cover is available, as in a frost-excluded greenhouse or sun-room, it is worth being more adventurous and perhaps including *Lippia citriodora*, the lemon-scented verbena, plumbago and oleander. Where tender plants are grown in pottery jars or other containers which it is impossible to fit with castors, it pays to have a little wheeled platform (raised 6 inches or so from the ground) on to which the containers can be lifted and trundled into shelter.

Clay pots are the most commonly seen of all containers. Up to about 12 inches in diameter, they are suitable for geraniums, lilies or spring bulbs. Larger pots from 12–25 inches are necessary for shrubs and trees. It is pleasant when it comes to choosing pots of this size to pick, where possible, some of the decorative Italian lemon pots or camellia vases. It is sometimes possible to buy large, rectangular, terra-cotta containers for spring bulbs or summer bedding plants to continue the theme.

Concrete pots and tubs are not really aesthetically satisfying as containers for shrubs and trees. Camellias and rhododendrons will not grow in them, and although one does see conifers and box trees sometimes grown in modern concrete containers styled to represent grey brick, studded with coloured tiles, they seldom look right, and one feels the plants would be happier with their roots in a cool clay pot or cosily ensconced in wood.

Concrete containers come into their own on a concrete terrace or patio when filled with gay summer annuals.

Wooden tubs and halved casks last longer if they are charred, or painted inside with Cuprinol Green—an excellent preservative which is harmless to plants. Wooden window boxes or troughs also last better if treated in a similar way.

Fibre-glass antique reproduction containers have the advantage of being very light in weight. The Verine range are beautifully moulded. The urns in Carolean, Georgian and Queen Anne designs include one by Robert Adam, another showing Italian/ Roman influences, and two very beautiful English styles with griffon handles and cherub heads. They would look splendid on top of a wall or balustrade or to flank a main entrance.

Tubs are offered in replicas of mediaeval, Tudor, Elizabethan, Georgian and Regency designs, and some of these are very beautiful, depicting galleons in full sail, nymphs and goats, St George and the dragon, lion masks and other subjects. With depths ranging from 11–18 inches, and widths up to 20 inches, they are ideal for camellias, scented rhododendrons, topiary shapes, pomegranates, Mexican orange, and other choice subjects. A replica of a James II lead tank, 30 inches deep and almost 5 feet long, may be used as a trough to accommodate a permanent planting of deep-rooting plants.

Free-standing troughs may be made of wood on the window box principle (see Chapter One) and fitted with feet to give stability. Deep troughs of this type are useful for permanent plantings of shrubs, ivy and periwinkle, while shallow ones can stand on low walls or within balcony railings offering homes to an assortment of spring bulbs followed by summer bedding.

Plain gateposts sometimes gain from being topped by shallow boxes made to fit, while plain, low walls can be made more attractive by the addition of wall boxes (Fig. 8).

Watering during holiday times can be a problem, as was pointed out in Part One, with reference to window boxes (see Chapter Two). Camplex Riviera Pots have now devised terrace troughs with a reservoir system to feed a linked system of troughs. This is particularly suitable for three or four troughs displayed on descending levels of staging against a wall, on a slope, or down a series of steps. All Riviera pots and troughs have built-in reservoirs which do away with the need of watering for two or three

Wall and gate-post containers in position

FIGURE 8.

weeks at a time. The reservoirs may be filled at one time from an ordinary tap, or they may be connected to a ball valve tank for completely automatic refilling.

Siting containers calls for careful thought. Too many containers in too small a space can give a restless, spotty effect. Moreover, in a very limited space, as on the balcony of a flat, a small terrace, stoep or sun-deck it is important to leave space for walking, sitting and above all room to tend the plants in comfort.

When planning containers for small balconies and stoeps, consideration should be given to the fixing of troughs to the railings, the use of cascade pots on the walls and hanging baskets overhead.

86

A metal saucepan stand, painted to fit in with the scheme, makes a useful and original stand for pots and, standing in the corner adjacent to the house, takes up little room.

In larger spaces, such as a yard or patio, it is important to create a feeling of unity. This is conveyed by using containers with the same visual association. The terrace of a country cottage might have white-painted barrels and tubs, and perhaps a wheelbarrow, in conjunction with white-painted, wooden window boxes. A Colt cedar or Lockwood wooden building would associate well with cedar or teak window boxes and modern-looking troughs and tubs, tongued and grooved in similar materials. On the other hand, a cement-paved patio or terrace with pierced concrete screening, would go well with tapered concrete containers and round concrete pots.

Much can be gained, too, from the artistic grouping of the containers and from variations in the shape and texture of the plantings. Larger terraces and patios benefit from the introduction of a focal feature such as a piece of statuary, a wall fountain or pool.

Contrast in the texture of the paving obtained by the use of cobbles or setts also helps to show off the pots. Where obtainable the use of glazed ceramic tiles set into the walls would help to create a sunny, Mediterranean atmosphere.

The grouping of the containers is all important. Informal arrangement of three or five pots to one side of a patio may be balanced by one diagonally placed on the other side with perhaps a wall-fountain, built-up boxed bed, or stone or lead figure at one end, flanked by a pot on each side and with wall-bracketed cascade pots arranged at different heights above the feature. Pots or urns might also stand on the coping (Fig. 9).

A change in levels can create additional interest. In Fig. 10 a large terra-cotta pitcher stands on a raised brick-built dais, surrounded by smaller pots of interesting shape, each on their own square pediment built of bricks. These are balanced by large pots at the right-hand side of the terrace while a similar pot, off-centre, in the left distance gives perspective.

Overcrowding must always be avoided if the patio or terrace is to have a restful, pleasing effect.

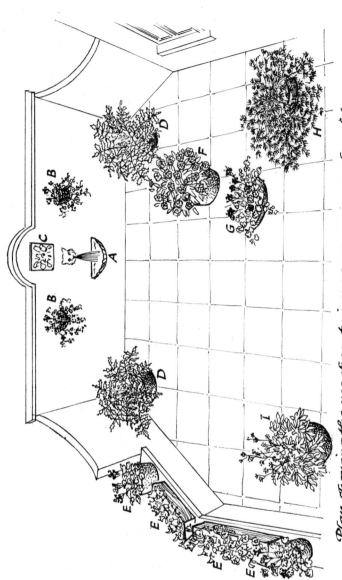

Plan showing the use of containers on a semi – enclosed terrace

A. Wall fountain with basin and lion's head.   B. Wall pots planted with ivy-leaved geraniums, variegated ivy or trailing lobelia.   C. Decorative tile.   D. Mahonias in pots.   E. Low wall with pots and boxes of geraniums, petunias, etc. on coping.   F. Camellia 'ADOLPHE AUDUSSON' in pot.   G. Low pot of ivy-leaved and Irene geraniums.   H. Dwarf maple ACER PALMATUM DISSECTUM ATROPURPUREUM in pot.   I. Castor-oil plant - FATSIA JAPONICA - in pot.

FIGURE 9.

88

Pot garden on terrace with french window leading from house

A. Urn of daffodils to be followed by geraniums on square brick pediment. B. Surrounding urns with BEGONIA FIMBRIATA each on low brick pediment. C. Pots of tulips, followed by petunias. D. Witch hazel for winter interest. E. 'Castor oil plant' FATSIA JAPONICA

FIGURE 10.

Border of white heaths

Path

Low wall with Pots of bulbs followed by summer flowers

Path

Roses underplanted with violas

White heaths

Low wall

89

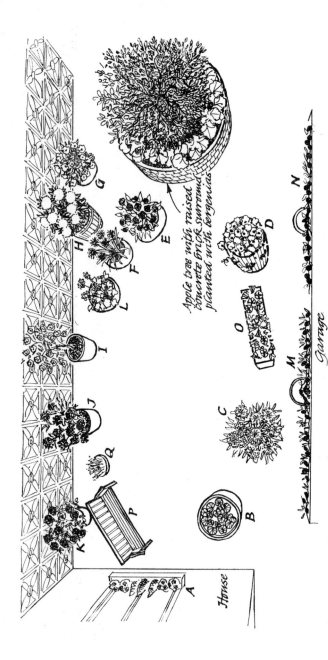

Apple tree with raised
concrete brick surround
planted with bergenias

Small yard or patio of modern semi—detached house

A. Window box. B. Water-lilies in tub. C. Lace-cap hydrangea in tub. D. Strawberry barrel.
E. Early tulips in tub followed by begonias. F. Hardy agapanthus. 'Headbourne hybrid.'
G. CAMELLIA 'ADOLPHE AUDUSSON' H. CHOISYA TERNATA in tub. I. Climbing rose 'Golden Showers'
in tub. J. SOLANUM CRISPUM 'Glasnevin' K. China rose 'Fellemberg' in tub. L. Narcissi 'April
Tears' and blue muscari, to be followed by ivy-leaved geraniums in tub. M. Espalier
trained 'Conference' pear. N. Peregrine peach in tub. O. Trough of miscellaneous spring bulbs
followed by pink, blue and white petunias. P. Seat. Q. Low tub of dwarf lavender.

FIGURE II.

90

It is important when choosing pots to demarc the limits of the terrace, or to stand on coping or steps, to make sure that they are big enough. Pots under 5 inches in diameter dry out too quickly. When choosing containers for bulbs, it is necessary to be sure that they are *deep* enough. By using a container 12–15 inches in depth it is possible to plant the bulbs in layers for successional flowering.

Fig. 11 shows how a small paved area at the rear of a semi-detached house can be transformed into an attractive patio by the

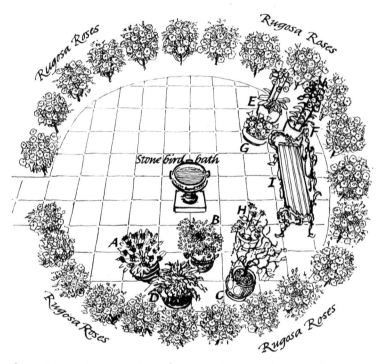

Paved sun-trap arbour in country with reproduction stone finished fibre glass pots containing:
A. VIBURNUM CARLESII B. Hydrangea, lace-cap variety
C. CORYLUS AVELLANA CONTORTA (Twisted hazel) D. JUNIPERUS
CHINENSIS 'Bluaw' E. Nicotiana in pot F. Lilies in pot
(Golden Clarion' strain) G. White petunias H. Ivy-leaved
geraniums in tub I. Reproduction wrought iron seat (painted white)

FIGURE 12.

use of tubs. Note how the central area has been left clear to make extra sitting space with room for children to tricycle or play with toys.

The water garden in a tub (Fig. 14) is fully explained in Chapter Fourteen, while Chapter Thirteen deals with the growing of fruit trees in tubs and pots.

Fig. 12 shows a treatment for a paved sitting-out area in a country garden. Here, sweetly-scented plants are sited near the seat, while a bird bath or figure make a focal point. Again a good area of paving is left clear to make room for deck chairs, table, and other garden furniture.

Most plants do well in plastic pots and there are fortunately many very reasonably priced plastic containers now available. Particularly useful are the large tree pots in green and black which can be used for bulbs (including lilies), stocks, begonias, fuchsias or pelargoniums as well as shrubs, climbers and small trees. White plastic urns have the advantage of being light in weight and look well on concrete paving.

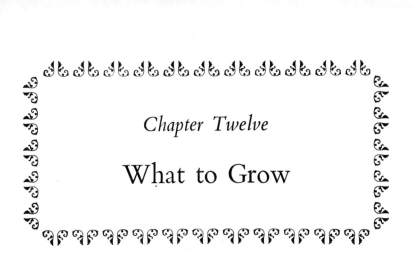

Chapter Twelve

What to Grow

All the plants recommended in Part One for window box use are suitable also for containers. In addition there is a wide choice of shrubs and trees that can be pot grown to grace any paved area within the garden (Fig. 13).

Perhaps the trees that most readily come to mind when one thinks of container-grown subjects are the mop-headed standards and Noah's-ark sentries of box that flank the entrances to some of the town-houses in the smarter districts of London. These can often be bought trained into the required shape from a large nursery firm such as Hillier's of Winchester.

The sweet bay (*Laurus nobilis*) is rather similar in use. Many of these little trees have been imported from Belgium, carefully clipped to the required shape. They usually arrive in very small containers and should be taken from these and potted into tubs 2 feet in diameter, or into half-barrels. Sweet bay is not fully hardy, so if the trees are to survive into old age they should be taken into a frost-proof greenhouse, sun-porch or even shed for the winter. They can then be trimmed each April before taking up their positions on the terrace or by the front door. Feeding helps and they should be topdressed with rotted manure or compost two or three times every year.

Watering of container-grown trees and shrubs is very important. They should never be allowed to dry out and to prevent

*JUNIPERUS COMMUNIS COMPRESSA
with it's columnar shape
makes a good container plant*

FIGURE 13.

this it pays to put a layer of rotted turves at the bottom and sides of the tubs.

When narrower, terra-cotta jars are used, the turf layer can go at the bottom. John Innes No. 3 suits most shrubs and trees, but lime-haters and fibrous-rooted subjects such as camellias, rhododendrons and azaleas, Japanese Maples and the like do better in the Royal Horticultural Society's recommended camellia compost. Both these mixtures are discussed in Chapter Three.

Birch trees are not often seen as pot-grown subjects, yet young sapling birches are most attractive to decorate terrace or patio with their slender grace and fresh lacy foliage. Norway maples, *Acer platanoides*, too, do well in pots and the dark-leafed form, *A. p.* 'Schwedleri', is particularly striking against a cream-coloured or whitewashed background. Fruit trees will be dealt with in the following chapter, but small ornamental trees of the cherry and apple families can be pleasing and I have seen young plants of the silver-leafed weeping pear, *Pyrus salicifolia* 'Pendula' doing well in tubs. If they are kept in smallish containers, the consequent root restriction keeps down the rate of growth and also ensures freedom of flowering. The compost in which they are grown must, however, be replenished by topdressing, and fertiliser should be added every year if it is not to become exhausted. The dainty Fuji cherry, *Prunus incisa*, makes a good subject for a tub or pot as does the bush form of the autumn cherry, *Prunus subhirtella*, of which the pink form, *rosea*, is rather less vigorous than the type and so more suitable for container use. It will, however, need consistent pinching out of the leading shoots in May and June if it is not to become too large. Such treatment also leads to an even greater profusion of the rosy crystal flowers it puts out during any mild spells from November until March.

For a really warm, sheltered patio, placed against a south wall, and especially if it can be appreciated from the house windows, one of the early Japanese apricot or plum cultivars would be delightful. One of the best of these is the crimson-flowered, hyacinth-scented *Prunus mume* 'Beni-shi-don', but many of the larger nurseries offer their own forms.

Camellias and scented rhododendrons will do well in such a situation, although in all but the mildest areas the more tender rhododendrons may have to be taken into shelter during frosty weather.

The camellia compost recommended by the R.H.S. is ideal for plants of this type. To grow camellias really well, half a shovelful of well-rotted cow manure should be added to each tubful of the compost. Dried blood and urea should also be fed from time to time. Watering is most important, particularly when the buds are enlarging, as drying out is a frequent cause of bud-drop. On the other hand, too much water will cause yellowing and falling of the leaves. It is essential to strike a happy medium.

With camellias and other choice plants, it is always a wise precaution to sink their pots into larger ornamental containers, filling the air space between with dry peat. This helps to protect the roots from frost.

It is not necessary to repot every year, although it is always advisable to 'pep up' the soil, topdressing with leafmould or rotted bracken and rotted cow manure. The plants flower more freely when not over-potted.

The buds and blooms of camellias and early-flowering rhododendrons, such as the pretty, milky white *R. leucaspis* and rosy 'Tessa', can be protected from frost if one puts a large brown paper bag (of the type for refuse collection or to enclose bedding) over the whole plant, weighting it to the ground with bricks. Brown paper gives much better protection than polythene but, of course, the bag must be removed as soon as the frost is over.

Good camellias for pot cultivation are 'Adolphe Audusson' (scarlet with showy gold stamens), 'Lady Clare' (rosy pink), 'Donation' (shell pink), 'J. C. Williams' (pale pink), and 'Lady Vansittart' (white striped pink). In Scotland and the far north of England, only 'Donation' and 'J. C. Williams' can be relied on to flower.

Of the tender, scented rhododendrons the hardiest for terrace and patio cultivation is the white *R. bullatum* with handsome crinkly foliage. Slightly more tender, but growing well against a wall in the south and west, 'Princess Alice' and 'Fragrantissimum' are worth a try.

Colourful and moderate-in-growth rhododendrons, without scent, are the cherry-coloured 'Humming Bird' with small, rounded, dark green leathery leaves, 'Bow Bells' pink, primrose yellow 'Diane' and terra-cotta 'Fabia' (which is later to bloom, flowering at the beginning of June and so missing the frost in cold areas).

Knaphill and Mollis azaleas are also pleasing in pots.

Really tender subjects which can spend the summer outdoors and at the same time greatly enhance the garden scene with their beauty are the oleanders which also make patio subjects *par excellence*, provided there is a cool greenhouse (from which frost is excluded by heating to 4–7°C (40–45°F) or a sun-porch or garden room able to offer similar protection. *Nerium oleander* with its lance-shaped, evergreen leaves and large clusters of small yet exotic blossoms, comes in single double varieties, and shades ranging from white through pale pink to rose and carmine. Yellow-flowered forms are also occasionally seen. Easy of cultivation they will do well in John Innes No. 3 and ask only to be protected from frost.

Datura suaveolens, the angel's trumpets, is a really spectacular shrubby plant for balcony or patio use. It needs a large pot or tub to accommodate its roots and, if well fed with any of the liquid fertilisers recommended in Chapter Two, will carry its great white trumpets almost continuously.

Near the open windows of a sitting room or on a terrace where one can sit out on a warm night, its exotic, heavy fragrance will be most appreciated.

The datura's only weakness is its attraction for red spider which suck the sap from the leaves until they turn yellow and drop off. Regular watering and a moist compost help to keep this trouble at bay, as does regular syringing of the leaves with warm water. Dusting with insecticide powder should be a routine precaution, but in spite of its proclivity to red spider infestation the datura will succeed easily so long as it is protected from frost in the winter. You can even dry it off and treat it much as you would treat a large, pot-grown fuchsia. If the leaves fall in winter it does not matter so long as frost is kept at bay. *Datura suaveolens* would, however, do even better if kept growing in a warm, moist greenhouse during the winter season.

Convolvulus mauritanicus is a low-growing, fairly tender shrubby trailer with pretty, harebell-mauve saucers. It can be blended with orange busy lizzie or the taller apricot-coloured semi-pendant *Mimulus aurantiacus* (syn. M. *glutinosus*) for an attractive scheme. Nearly hardy, both the convolvulus and mimulus will survive for years if wintered in a light, frost-proof place.

Aster pappei is a glorious, half-hardy daisy with low mounds of fresh green foliage and bright blue, gold-centred daisies. It is an appealing eye-catcher to plant at the base of a half-standard fuchsia (especially one with pale pink and deep blue flowers), and both can winter under frost-excluded glass without disturbance. If no light and frost-proof shelter is available, sacrifice the aster plants—having arranged for their renewal by cuttings struck in warmth and brought on in the window of an unheated room. The fuchsia will survive the winter if stored in a frost-free shed or garage and kept fairly dry (watering only every 10 or 12 days). In late April it should be brought out, repotted, its head of branchlets snipped back, well watered and brought into the light to start into growth.

Watering of pot plants is most important during the summer months, and most will need filling up to the rim of their containers every day during hot weather. To replace the nourishment which the watering leaches from the soil, give a feed of liquid manure every week or ten days from June on.

Hardy subjects are particularly useful, and apart from the birches, Norway maple, cherries, hardier rhododendrons and camellias mentioned earlier in the chapter, useful shrubs would be the variegated elaeagnus, *E. pungens* 'Maculata', small maples such as the purple-leafed *Acer palmatum* 'Atropurpureum', and the slower-growing A. *p.* 'Dissectum' with its attractive, lacily-cut foliage. Evergreen azaleas are useful for small tubs and the hydrangeas, especially the appealingly patterned 'lace-cap' varieties, are very effective.

Troughs of heaths, or low square containers similarly planted, especially those calluna varieties which combine coloured foliage with their flower appeal, are useful. Good cultivars would be the orange-umber-foliaged 'Robert Chapman' and 'Gold Haze'. These would combine well with the striking double-lavender, rosetted flowers of 'Elsie Purnell'.

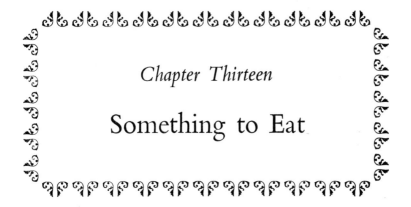

Chapter Thirteen

Something to Eat

The prime function of containers on the garden terrace or stoep, in the patio or on the balcony is to enable one to grow decorative plants to delight the eye. Most of us, however, also enjoy growing things to eat and often these can be as full of eye-appeal as any of the ornamentals.

Strawberry barrels are an idea to delight both eye and palate, particularly when planted with perpetual-fruiting varieties such as 'Sans Rivale' or 'Gento'.

Strawberry barrels can be started whenever the plants can be obtained. Sometimes it is possible to buy them purpose made. Otherwise you can procure a sound barrel and bore 1-inch holes at about 18-inch intervals—the more irregular the spacing, the more decorative the effect.

Bore drainage holes at the base of the barrel and fix castors to the bottom so that you can move it easily if it is to stand on paving or concrete. Strawberry barrels require efficient drainage, so it is important to put a 6-inch layer of broken crocks at the bottom. They need a central core of drainage, too, and this is most easily provided by putting a piece of piping or small drainpipe in the middle, filling it with rubble and gradually raising it to allow the material to trickle into position as the soil is added.

Any good garden soil is suitable but the addition of well-moistened peat with 2 oz of bonemeal laced through the mixture will ensure better crops of strawberries, otherwise use John Innes No. 3. As the soil reaches the level of the holes poke in the plants, firming them well before adding more.

A properly made and planted strawberry barrel will go on for years, each season yielding heavier crops. Pottery strawberry crocks or 'holed pots' are also sometimes available and are equally decorative in effect.

Window boxes may be planted with strawberries and perpetual-fruiting strawberries may also be set in hanging baskets, allowing their runners to trail prettily down.

The secret of success lies in removing the first flush of blossom to give the plants a chance to settle down and build themselves up before fruiting. Watering, too, is important and an occasional feed of liquid manure will help to ensure flavoursome crops.

Runner beans do well in containers. A low tub or half-barrel is ideal and the beans can be trained up a tripod of poles or a central pole or cane supporting a 'wigwam' of twine looped over hooks on the rim of the container. The beans need plenty of moisture while they are growing, so to prevent drying out it is worth lining the base and sides of the container with several thicknesses of newspaper soaked well in water. Good garden soil is the best growing medium for pot-grown vegetables but for flat dwellers and those without gardens this may be almost impossible to come by. They will find, however, that John Innes No. 2, available in small bags from the multiple stores and many sundriesmen in spring, mixed with peat, will give good results.

The peat should be moist before use, and an easy way to ensure this is to stab holes in its polythene bag and immerse it overnight in a bucket or sink of water, squeezing out the surplus moisture before use.

Runner beans need a generous diet and it pays to incorporate some well-rotted manure in the compost if you can get it. Sacks of rotted stable manure are sometimes sold and will give good results. Failing this, use a good general fertiliser. The seed should be set a foot apart and 3 inches deep in May. Dwarf beans may be sown 8 inches apart in a double row around the edge of the container. They may also be grown in a trough set against a wall with a panel of Netlon plastic mesh for support.

Fruit trees in pots are a rewarding and decorative proposition for the container gardener. Twelve-inch pots are the most suitable for young trees, but after a few years they will need to be repotted in 18-inch pots and can then be expected to go on and fruit for 20 years or more.

Pot-grown bush-trees can be bought, but are expensive and it is just as satisfactory and much more interesting to buy two-year-old maidens and train them oneself. When ordering, it is important to let the nurseryman know that the trees are for pot work so that he will be sure to supply trees grafted on suitable dwarfing stock.

Tried and tested varieties for pot work include apples 'Charles Ross', 'Laxton's Superb' and 'Cox's Orange Pippin'; 'William's Bon Chrétien' or 'Doyenné de Comice' pears; 'Victoria' plum; 'Moorpark' apricot and 'Peregrine' or 'Hale's Early' peaches. It is sometimes possible to buy 'Family Trees with two or three varieties of apple grafted on to the same tree.

A good compost for fruit trees can be made up of:

3 parts fibrous loam
1 part well-rotted manure
A handful of bonemeal per pot
A little ground chalk

The pots should be well soaked before planting the trees.

Crock the pots well with broken crockery or large stones, then add a shovelful of compost. Stand the young trees on this, spreading out the roots and cut back any damaged or straggly ones. Add the soil gradually, tamping it firm with the handle of the trowel.

Where possible, it helps to sink the pots into the ground during the winter to avoid frost damage. Where this cannot be done, cover the compost with a 2-inch layer of dry peat and then encase the pots in sacking or two or three layers of black polythene to protect them during the winter, removing it in late spring when frost danger is over.

In the first spring the trees will probably need little pruning, although young peaches and apricots may benefit from having young, unripe green wood cut back. Any damaged twigs should, of course, be cut off when planting.

All flower buds should be removed during the first season, and particular attention should be paid to watering.

Pinch off any inward-growing shoots or long, sappy shoots.

In late July, using finger and thumb, pinch back all side shoots to the fifth or sixth leaf.

In November top up the pots with fresh compost before sacking them up for the winter.

Some of the trees may flower the following spring and may be allowed to bear their first crops. This will increase their water-need, as dryness at the roots may cause the fruit to drop. They will need extra feeding, too, and all trees carrying fruit should be fed with liquid manure twice a week.

In July, repeat the previous year's pruning, nipping back all side shoots to five leaves and just tipping back the main branches. Remove any too-long growth. Summer pruning of this kind increases the fruit yield as well as building up shapely trees. Once the main framework is established and the trees are as big as you want them to be, pruning can be more severe, cutting back the leaders to a third their length, and spur-pruning by tipping all side shoots back to a couple of buds in July and then cutting them back again in winter, thus removing any secondary growth at the same time. As with roses, always make a slanting cut, and prune to an outside bud, keeping the centre open.

Pests and diseases must be controlled. Aphis on peaches and apples may be troublesome and should be sprayed as necessary. Spraying Hexyl Plus when in bud is one of the best ways to control insect pests.

Peaches and nectarines are subject to peach leaf curl, and should be sprayed with Dithane in mid-February and again in autumn. All red and blistered leaves should be picked off and burned.

Mildew sometimes infects apples and pears, and any affected trees should be sprayed with dinocap as soon as the white, powdery mould appears, having first cut off the diseased parts.

Birds and wasps may be a nuisance and it pays to tie individual polythene bags over the fruits as they reach the ripening stage.

Do not let the trees overcrop at first. Apples, pears, plums, peaches and apricots should not be allowed to ripen more than three or four fruits the first year. The quantity may be increased each year, but no tree under six years old should be allowed to bear more than two dozen fruit. After that they will be strong enough to carry all they produce as, in any case the trees themselves tend to drop the surplus without human interference.

Each autumn, some of the old compost should be scraped away and replenished with fresh. Every third year, the trees should be pulled out of the pots and their roots similarly scraped free of some of the old compost before being repotted in fresh. Any thick tap roots should be cut away before repotting.

Peaches, apricots and the 'Victoria' plum are self-fertile as is the 'Conference' pear. Most other varieties need a suitable pollinator, for this reason 'Laxton's Superb' apple and 'Cox's Orange Pippin' should be grown together and 'Conference' should always be included along with any other pear to pollinate it. 'Family Trees' usually have their varieties chosen so that they will pollinate each other.

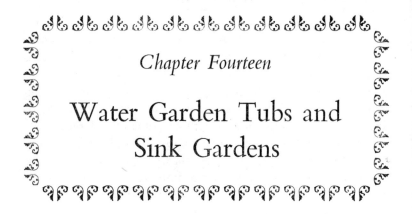

Chapter Fourteen

Water Garden Tubs and Sink Gardens

Water adds enchantment to any garden—and nowhere more so than in a patio, on a terrace, roof-garden, backyard or corner of a balcony. Even if the sparkle and splash of a fountain seems out of the question on grounds of expense it is still possible to add the charm of water by making a garden in a tub.

Making a tub water garden is not difficult. Any watertight half-cask, half-barrel or tub will do, or you can buy one of the fibre glass reproduction troughs or pots that appeals to you, and either plug the drainage holes with watertight mastic, or ask to be supplied with a container without holes. Even an ordinary green plastic plant tub will do, provided the drainage hole is sealed.

If you are using a cask see that the inside is properly charred, as described on p. 83.

June is the best time to plant a water garden but with care many subjects can be moved at most times of the year. Before planting, place a 5-inch layer of heavy loam, well mixed with bonemeal at the bottom. Let it settle and then trickle in the water very slowly to avoid churning up the bottom.

Naturally you will want a water-lily and here it is important to pick a variety that is not too strong growing and does not need too great a depth of water. Most tubs and containers used for water gardens are about 18 inches deep.

A mini-lily that is very suitable for tub cultivation is the sweet-smelling *Nymphaea odorata minor* with waxy-white, water-lily blooms centred with golden stamens.

Nymphaea 'Laydekeri Lilacea' is a pretty pink lily with carmine spots that will also do well under tub conditions. So will the flamboyant red *N.* 'L. Fulgens'. Tinier, with blooms little bigger than a tenpenny piece but carrying sixty or more flowers in a summer, are the miniature white *N. pygmaea alba* and the primrose-yellow *N.* × *p. helvola* with dark, mottled, glossy little pads of leaves.

All water-lilies need soil in which to grow. They can be planted in small plastic pots or fruit-punnets of the kind in which raspberries and strawberries are sold, with a piece of turf placed upside down over the roots and bound into position with string.

Water must be oxygenated if it is to be kept clean and fresh, so it is necessary to include one or two oxygenating plants like the water-violet, *Hottonia palustris*, the water-hawthorn, *Aponogeton distachyus*, or *Sagittaria japonica*, with stock-like, double white flowers and attractive arrow-shaped leaves.

Tubs can also be sunk into the soil in a lawn or border. When this is done, the rim should be disguised by flat stones. This will give a cue to the marginal plants that will help to blend the tub garden in with its surroundings. These are planted in pockets, made by building up small rocks at the edge of the tub to within about 4 inches of the surface of the water. Wedge small pots containing the plants into the top layer, or make small pockets as shown in the illustration (Fig. 14). In the pockets, plant the water forget-me-not *Myosotis palustris*, the magnificent pink iris—*Iris laevigata* 'Rose Queen' or the wild yellow flag of British streams. Among the stones at the edge you might add the golden marsh marigold, *Caltha palustris*, or one of the tall-stemmed, water-loving candelabra primulas, *Primula japonica* (red or pink) or *P. sikkimensis* (yellow).

Fish may also be added. Your local pet shop will advise you here about the number and type that you can comfortably keep, according to the size of the tub.

A miniature alpine garden that will give a great deal of pleasure can be constructed in a trough or sink—until the full possibilities of these little gardens were widely realised, it used to be possible to pick up old stone sinks from builders' demolition yards, and to buy stone or slate drinking troughs from country farms and small-holdings. North Wales, the Cotswolds and the north of England were rewarding hunting grounds for treasures of this type and an old friend of ours, gardening in a Welsh valley, even had the slate coffin of a Welsh prince to house his androsaces, tiny saxifrages, *Rosa roulettii* and other mini-fascinations.

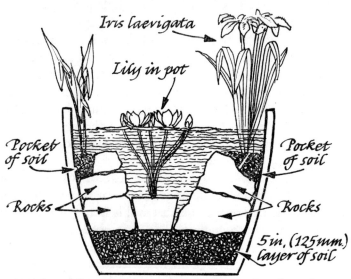

Iris laevigata

Lily in pot

Pocket of soil

Pocket of soil

Rocks

Rocks

5 in. (125 mm.) layer of soil

Section of water garden in a tub showing water lily in plastic pot or basket, showing method of placing rocks to form marginal pockets of soil in which to plant semi-aquatics

FIGURE 14.

Modern but genuine stone troughs made by craftsmen can still be bought from stone-masons and some garden centres, especially in the Cotswolds and the Lake District—at a price. It is not too difficult, however, to make one from concrete and, given a rough finish and washed over, when dry, with a solution of sulphate of iron it will have at least the superficial appearance of weathered brown stone.

To construct a sink it is first necessary to form a mould, consisting of two wooden boxes, one slightly smaller than the other to allow at least $1\frac{1}{2}$ inches thickness for the walls of the trough.

In the first instance, pour liquid concrete into the bottom of the larger box to a depth of $1\frac{1}{2}$–2 inches to form the base. Provision should be made for drainage holes by placing wooden plugs in the desired positions beforehand. The concrete will then set round these.

The surface of both boxes and of the plugs should be well smeared with soft soap to facilitate their removal when the concrete has set.

To give the trough extra strength, a sheet of wire netting bent into the shape of a shallow tray should be incorporated in the bottom. Stout wires bent into right angles should be used to reinforce the corners.

When the base of the larger box is filled with cement, the smaller box should be placed in position, resting on the drainage plugs which should be flush with the surface of the concrete.

The walls are formed by pouring more concrete into the space between the two boxes until the required height is reached. When the concrete has set properly the boxes and plugs are removed, leaving the trough *in situ*.

Care should be taken to see that the gravel used in the concrete mixture is not too coarse, otherwise it may jam between the boxes, causing a flaw.

A concrete mixture containing fine grit in addition to the usual cement and sand will give a more attractive finish.

Wiping over with water in which rice has been boiled gives a sticky surface to encourage moss and lichens to grow and so give an aged appearance.

Before planting, the inside of the trough should be soaked with a solution of permanganate of potash to counteract any ill effects of the cement on the plants.

Drainage is vital to the success of alpine plants, as stagnant moisture causes damping off round the collar or else rots the fragile roots, and the plants subsequently die.

It is important, then, to see that the drainage holes are crocked with a concave piece of broken flower-pot and that the container is filled with pieces of broken crock or small stones to a quarter of its depth.

A layer of roughage should be spread over the drainage material to prevent the soil being washed down among the crocks. Really coarse peat or the stalks of rotted bracken are excellent for this purpose (Fig. 15).

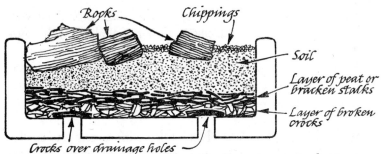

Sink for alpines. Section shows method of drainage and the positioning of rocks

FIGURE 15.

A good alpine compost consists of:

4 parts good loam (sieved)
2 of peat (or leafmould)
2 of sharp sand
1 of coarse grit (limestone chicken grit is suitable for lime-loving plants, but for lime-haters use granite chips instead).

The compost should be turned over and over until all the ingredients are thoroughly mixed. It should then be sprinkled with water from a fine-rosed can and turned again so that it becomes uniformly moist.

The compost should then be poured into the trough to about half its depth. At this stage the rocks should be added, choosing two or three characterful pieces, and taking care to give them a backward tilt and ensure that the strata run the same way, in all, to give them a natural effect. Place the rocks to give the effect of a

108

natural outcrop. Then fill up with compost to cover them for two-thirds their size, adding smaller rocks of the same type, and placing them as they might appear in nature. Try to construct pockets and crevices, adding the plants as you build. If you can get some pieces of tufa stone, these will add extra interest—with ready-made crevices and holes bored into the stone in which compact, cushion-forming saxifrages and other similar subjects can be planted.

When planting, the compost in the crevices should be firmly packed, being wedged into position with flakes of stone.

It helps to give the impression of a landscape in miniature, if one includes one or two really dwarf conifers—planting a prostrate one at the top of the outcrop and an upright-growing columnar form at the base of a little cliff. *Chamaecyparis obtusa* 'Caespitosa', *C. o.* 'Minima', *C. o.* 'Juniperoides' or *C. pisifera* 'Nana' would do well to plant at the apex of the outcrop, while the slim pencil-shape of *Juniperus communis* 'Compressa' cannot be beaten as an upright sentinel form at the base of a tiny cliff.

A topdressing of stone chippings should be spread over the surface of the compost after planting. The chippings help to keep the damp away from the crowns of the plants in winter, and in summer they act as a mulch to retain the moisture in the soil and prevent it drying out. Limestone chicken grit can be used, unless lime-hating plants are being grown, when granite chips should be chosen in preference.

Suitable plants for a trough garden include *Aethionema* 'Warley Rose', *Androsace lanuginosa* (pink-flowered rock jasmine), *A. sempervivoides* (pink flowers on glossy green rosettes), *A. villosa* and *A. v. arachnoidea* (white flowers on silvery, woolly tuffets), *Armeria caespitosa* 'Alba' (tiny white thrift), *Asperula suberosa* (silver foliage and tiny pink trumpets), *Campanula arvatica* (violet stars), *C. pulla* (purple bells), *Dianthus freynii* (tiny 'pinks'), *Erinus alpinus* 'Mrs Charles Boyle' (carmine stars), *Genista pilosa* (a small broom), *Gentiana verna* (bright blue gentians), *Geranium napuligerum* (*syn. G. farreri*) (apple-blossom pink saucers), *Gypsophila* 'Fratensis' (close grey carpet with pink flowers), *Houstonia caerulea* (lavender-blue little flowers should be given a damp spot), *Iris lacustris* (tiny irises—lavender-blue, gold-crested), *Polygala calcarea* (brilliant blue milkwort), *Raoulia australis* (silver mats), saxifrage such as 'Aubrey Pritchard' (grey rosettes, rosy-mauve flowers), *burseriana* (grey, spiny cushions, white flowers), 'Faldonside' (spiny grey rosettes, sulphur yellow flowers), 'Iris Pritchard' (grey rosettes, apricot flowers), *jenkinsiae* (grey-green cushions, very pretty dark-eyed, pink flowers), *Salix boydii* (attractive dwarf willow), *Silene acaulis* (green domes cushioned with pink flowers), *Soldanella alpina* (fringed, lavender-blue bells), *Veronica bombycina* (woolly white leaves, pale blue flowers), *Viola blanda* (sweetly-scented white violets), *V. labradorica* 'Purpurea' (bronze leaves and purple violets), *Edraianthus pumili.* (silver-grey leaves, upturned lavender-blue bells).

Tiny bulbous plants such as *Crocus ancyrensis* 'Golden Bunch', *Narcissus cylamineus* and the 'Hoop-petticoat', *N. bulbocodium*, species tulips such as *dasystemon* and *hageri*, and the snake's-head fritillaries—*Fritillaria meleagris*—are also suitable. It is important, however, to be selective and not to overplant, or the charm will be lost and the effect become simply a muddle.

Among the many uses of container-grown plants, one should not overlook the possiblity of bringing on bulbs, tender perennials such as geraniums or the moisture-loving astilbes and colourful annuals, such as the miniature cypress-like kochia which turns to burning-bush-like flames of scarlet and crimson, to plunge into the borders and bridge the various gaps that occur during the flowering season—in June when the easy lily hybrids are at their peak; in early August when the geraniums and astilbes function together with the glorious *Lilium auratum* cultivars, or in autumn when pot-grown chrysanthemums and the kochias can give a harvest glow.

Lilies as container plants, however, have a leading part to play, quite apart from this utility rôle when, in green plastic tubs, handsome pots of reconstituted stone, or the antique Verine reproductions, they can bring a touch of real glamour to patio, terrace or stoep.

Lilies take well to pot cultivation. They are often longer lived and healthier when container grown than when fighting off fungus and pest invasions in the open border. In pots, too, there is less risk of waterlogged conditions in winter to rot the bulbs.

Particularly suitable are the hybrids and cultivars of *auratum, candidum, dauricum, hansonii, henryi, longiflorum, speciosum, testaceum* and *tigrinum.* Exceptionally good are the hybrids 'Enchantment' and 'Limelight', hybrids of the 'Fiesta' strain and 'Mid-Century' and 'Oriental' hybrids. *Lilium regale* and the trumpet lilies of the 'Royal Gold' and 'Pink Perfection' strain also do well.

Lily compost should consist of two-thirds fibrous loam and one-third well-rotted leafmould, adding plenty of builder's coarse sand, and a few pieces of charcoal to keep the mixture sweet. Good drainage is essential, so it is important to see that the pots are well crocked.

Pot the bulbs as soon as received, three to a 15-inch pot or tub. Or the bulbs may be potted individually in 6-inch pots and later sunk together into a large container or in groups in the border. I prefer, however, to plant three bulbs together in one of the larger pots, setting them as far as possible from each other and standing the base of each on a pinch of sand.

The bulbs should be firmly potted, barely covering their tops and leaving room to add more compost when the stem roots appear.

Protection should be given until frost danger is past and this can be achieved by parcelling the containers in black polythene to 'plunge' them, or by standing them under a north-facing wall or hedge (north in the northern hemisphere only, of course) on a bed of weathered ashes to prevent the pots standing in pools of stagnant moisture, and mounding peat fibre or old leafmould over the pots to keep off frost and excessive rain. Remove this cover in April; move the pots to a sunny position and start to water them sparingly. Topdress as the stem roots appear and keep adding compost until it is just below the level of the top.

Clematis are among the most satisfactory climbers for pot or tub cultivation. They may either be trained on plastic-mesh cylinders surrounding the container, be housed in tubs standing against a wall and trained up trellis or plastic-mesh panels (Netlon or Gro-Mesh) fixed to the wall, or grown in tall Ali-Baba-type jars and allowed to flop over and embower the container.

John Innes No. 3 compost (see Chapter Two) should be used, with additional liquid feeds throughout the growing season, and the container must never be allowed to dry out. The compost surface should be removed and topdressed with fresh compost every

year, and after five or six years may need repotting in a fresh
mixture altogether. So long as they flower well and look healthy
however, clematis should be allowed to remain undisturbed.

Clematis need a cool root run and for this reason it helps to
grow an undemanding floppy subject in the same pot to shade the
roots. Catmint (nepeta) or the blue, hardy *Geranium grandiflorum*
are ideal.

Non-rampant but hardy and easily-pleased varieties are the
ones to choose. The striped pale-pink and rose 'Nelly Moser',
purple-blue 'Lord Balfour', violet 'President', rose-pink 'Com-
tesse de Bouchaud' and lavender-blue 'Mrs Cholmondely' will
all give good results.

Other climbers needing similar conditions are the lovely blue
and white hardy passion flower, *Passiflora caerulea*, *Mutisia retusa*,
a scrambler from Chile with large, glistening pale pink daisies,
Solanum crispum with blue and gold potato flowers, and a floppy
habit of growth and the various jasmines.

Nasturtiums also look pretty when grown in a tall jar and
allowed to trail and cascade over the edge.

Bonsai—Japanese-style, dwarfed trees are attractive container
subjects, and three or four specimens strategically placed can help
to give character to a patio or balcony.

Bonsai are full-scale trees, dwarfed by the pruning of their roots,
and patiently trained to create picturesque, windswept effects. It
is now possible to buy ready-dwarfed, trained trees in suitable
containers. Alternatively, one can train one's own, buying two- or
three-year-old plants or raising them from seed. Even quite large
plants of some species can be dwarfed to occupy small containers,
giving an appearance of great age.

I know of a *Taxodium distichum*, swamp cypress, brought in from
an American nursery when 9 feet tall and cut back almost to the
bottom branches. Its roots were shortened and it was repotted
into an 18-inch tub in which it spent the summer.

The following spring it was lifted from its pot and the roots
were again pruned back. Again the next year the process was
repeated, and roots the thickness of a thumb were sawn off. At the
same time the top was again pruned, leaving a double leader

arising from the cut-back top. The following year one of the leaders was removed, giving the original cut-back portion the effect of having been struck by lightning.

By systematic pinching back and snipping-out of unwanted shoots and by yearly root pruning the desired artistic effect was achieved.

Good plants for Bonsai treatment are beech and birch seedlings, forsythia, ginkgo, Japanese azalea, Japanese maples, oak, *Wisteria floribunda*, *Cedrus atlantica glauca*, *Juniperus chinensis* and *J. procumbens*, winter jasmine and *Prunus incisa*. Chaenomeles (*Cydonia*) also make attractive specimens. The conifers have the advantage of remaining evergreen, but the flowering trails of mauve or white wisteria, the golden stars of jasmine and scarlet quince blossoms decorating the gnarled branches are picturesque in the extreme.

The principles of Bonsai cultivation are as follows:

The containers should be shallow oval, round or oblong pans, glazed on the outside and not much deeper than 2 inches on the inside so as to restrict the roots. They must have one or more drainage vents.

Drainage must be perfect as the plants need plenty of water, and unless the surplus soaks rapidly away from the surface it will cause the roots to rot.

A concave crock (not a flat stone) must be placed over each vent and the pan filled to a quarter its depth with fine gravel or coarse grit. The gritty material should be covered with a film of granulated peat, just sufficient to prevent the compost washing down and clogging the drainage.

The compost for Bonsai specimens should be made up as follows:

2 parts (all parts by volume) old fibrous loam rubbed down between the hands
1 part of sieved leafmould
2 parts of coarse sand,
a dusting of bonemeal

For conifers use 3 parts of sand.

When planting, place a layer of compost over the granulated

peat and sit the tree upon it at one end of the pan, carefully spreading out the roots and working the compost between them. Add enough compost just to reach the base of the trunk, mounding it at that end and, if possible, showing a little of the thickest root.

Root pruning (See Fig. 16) should be carried out yearly. This applies to all types of tree except pines, which must never have their roots cut or they bleed to death. In their case, just pull away any dead roots, and wind any over-long healthy roots around the base of the trunk and tie them in a knot.

Branch pruning and shaping should be carried out with slanting cuts, removing shoots so that those left balance each other and maintain a picturesque shape (Fig. 16).

Seedling trees are easy to train. Planted in small pots when 5 or 6 inches high they may be controlled easily by the pinching out of surplus growth buds. The Japanese train the trees with wire, but sufficient shape to satisfy Western taste can usually be obtained without resort to this, either by the removal of growth buds or cutting back with nail-clippers on the lines shown in the diagram p. 116.

Transplanting should be carried out each spring until the little trees attain the desired height and shape. Pot them on gradually into larger pots until a strong system of fibrous roots has developed when they are ready to go into their permanent containers. If a tap root develops, cut it back half-way and remove it completely the following year. The aim is gradually to remove all the main, thick roots and to get the tree growing entirely on fibrous feeding roots. After root pruning and repotting, water the tree and keep it protected from wind and sun until it is re-established.

Half-shade, away from tree drip, suits Bonsai best. Watering should be carried out once a day, except in very hot weather, when the plants should be watered twice.

In winter the trees should be moved into a cool greenhouse or frost-proof room or shed. Once established they are quite hardy but the containers might crack in heavy frost.

Standard wisterias may be trained and will make lovely terrace or patio plants. They need very heavy containers though, as having considerable 'sail-area' they tend to be blown over by the wind.

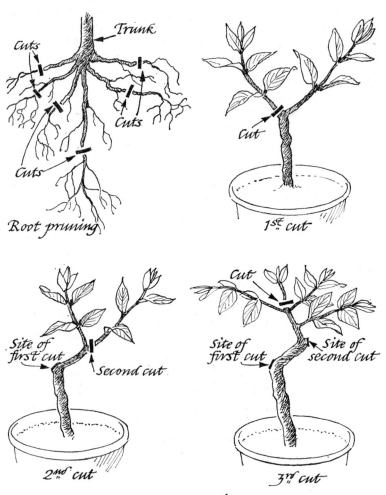

Trunk

Cuts

Cuts

Cuts

Root pruning

Cut

1ˢᵗ cut

Site of first cut

Second cut

2ⁿᵈ cut

Cut

Site of first cut

Site of second cut

3ʳᵈ cut

Semi–diagrammatic drawing to illustrate the root and shoot pruning of a Bonsai specimen in order to build up an attractive shape from a seedling tree

FIGURE 16.

The young wisteria plant, purchased in spring, should be knocked out of its pot and planted in the container, its roots being just teased out. John Innes No. 3 compost is used for planting, and it is wise to untie the plant from its nursery cane and insert a strong stake (the light aluminium dipole from a discarded TV aerial is very useful). I like to place a couple of heavy stones strategically over the root area to wedge against the stake and hold it firm in the compost.

The first summer one should pinch back all side shoots to three buds. Repeat the process the following year, and in subsequent years pinch back to two buds.

After three years the plant will begin to flower, and by five years it will have built up into a most attractive little tree with arching weeping branches.

I usually allow two or three main stems to intertwine to give added strength, stopping the top-growth at 3 or 5 feet, according to requirement.

Provided the plant is topdressed with fresh compost and the soil stirred each autumn, the wisteria should grow satisfactorily in the same container for years.

The secret of growth control in pot-grown shrubs is constant watchfulness, pinching back or pinching out unwanted shoots or buds before they give trouble. In this way quite large shrubs can easily be kept within bounds.

Roses will grow well in pots, thus offering their admirers a chance to grow and enjoy them, even where they have no garden. Roof-gardens, balconies, stoeps, entrance porches, yards and patios all offer them a home.

Suitable cultivars of hybrid tea roses for outdoor pot cultivation include: 'Karl Herbst' (strawberry red), 'Lady Sylvia' (warm flesh pink), 'Spek's Yellow', 'Super Star' (vermilion), 'Wendy Cussons' (cerise-pink), and 'Josephine Bruce' (crimson).

Among the floribundas a good choice would be: 'All Gold', 'Dearest' (pink), 'Evelyn Fison' (scarlet-crimson), 'Iceberg' (white), 'Lilac Charm' (single lavender), 'Orangeade' (semi-single orange-scarlet), and 'Spartan' (salmon-orange).

Ten-inch pots should be selected, or other containers of a

similar size. They must be deep enough to allow the bushes to form a vigorous root system.

A humus-containing compost such as John Innes No. 3 with additional peat should be used. Otherwise make up a mixture of:

$\frac{1}{3}$ rotted turf
$\frac{1}{3}$ rotted manure
$\frac{1}{3}$ loamy garden soil

The roses should have all their vigorous shoots cut back by a third when they are potted up in autumn. Any damaged roots should be removed, and any dead or torn wood cut out. If possible they should spend the winter in the shelter of a cold greenhouse, sun-porch, or cold frame, or have their pots sunk to the rim in the soil in a sheltered place. Where this is not possible, protect the pots and roots with sacking or heavy-duty polythene.

Prune in March, cutting back the shoots with a cut slanting away back from an outward-facing bud. The severity of the pruning depends upon the variety and vigour of the rose. Pruning of vigorous roses in pots is usually more severe than if they are left in the open ground. Cut the strong-growing varieties to about $1\frac{1}{2}$–2 feet from the soil level, and shorten back the weaker roses to a foot.

Watering is important, as dryness at the roots will be conducive to mildew infection.

Spray against mildew and black spot at the first sign of trouble, using a systemic such as Benlate and repeating after a one-week interval. Spraying with a good insecticide against white fly, greenfly and thrips should be carried out in April and repeated at fortnightly intervals or when necessary.

Remove all dead blooms, shortening the stems back to an outward-facing bud and taking care to keep the centre of the bush open.

Feeding is necessary for pot-grown roses, and a liquid feed such as Liquinure should be given at 10-day intervals.

Topdress in the autumn with fresh compost, scraping away some of the old. Pot-grown roses should be repotted every two years or they will exhaust the compost.

Chapter Sixteen

Hanging Baskets

Hanging baskets, I think, deserve a chapter of their own because, not only do they present their own particular problems in planting and management, but they have a special charm, and—particularly where there is very little actual garden—confer a pleasant and flowery atmosphere on balconies, loggias, stoeps and entrance porches. Outside shops, restaurants and town-houses they bring a breath of the country and help very much to brighten and make attractive the surroundings.

It is often expensive to buy ready-made-up baskets, but one can usually purchase the wire frame from a garden shop or good ironmonger.

The best type of basket is the common round, galvanised-wire one. Plastic ones are more artificial looking, and the square ones that are sometimes seen somehow do not seem to have quite the charm of the traditional pudding-bowl shape.

To conserve moisture, the basket may be lined either with black polythene, which does the job well and is quite unobtrusive, or with sphagnum moss which has the advantage, if well watered, of remaining green and growing.

John Innes No. 2 compost, which can be bought ready mixed, is perhaps the most satisfactory for hanging baskets, though I like to add extra peat to help to retain the moisture. It is important, however, that the peat should be thoroughly soaked before use, otherwise it will absorb water from the rest of the compost, and so deprive the plants of moisture, rather than acting as a reservoir which should be the aim.

Ivy-leafed 'geraniums' are among the most suitable and widely used plants. Of these the pale pink 'Mme Crousse', the deeper 'Galilee' and lilac 'Mrs Martin' or 'La France' and tyrian purple 'Abel Carrière' are excellent, with 'L'Elegante' added for the attraction of its cream-edged, pink-tinged leaves as much as for its shapely white flowers.

Fuchsias again are a 'natural' on account of their graceful pendant flowers. For this purpose the plants are best raised from cuttings rooted in September and overwintered in 3-inch pots. Fuchsia plants for hanging baskets should be freely branching, so the growing points should be pinched out when they are 2 or 3 inches high. The resultant side shoots should then be pinched back when they in turn reach this length and the result will be cascading mounds of colour that are ideal for use in hanging baskets. Good varieties are 'Cascade', 'White Spider', 'Red Spider', 'Marinka' and 'Dusky Rose'.

Trailing lobelia associates well with most other plants used for hanging baskets. It can even be used alone and, set in well-enriched compost, and thickly planted, will give the impression of a flowering ball of gentian blue. 'Sapphire' is a good variety to choose and the plants may be sown in heat in January or early February (16 °C (60 °F) is the temperature at which they will most readily germinate if you have the use of a mini-propagator). They should be pricked out into boxes or Jiffy pots as soon as they are big enough to handle, pricking them out in tiny clumps rather than individual seedlings.

The campanula family offers two lovely trailers to join the ivy-leafed pelargoniums, fuchsias and lobelias in decorating hanging baskets. They are the starry-eyed *C. isophylla* with its cultivars 'Mayi' in blue and the snowy-white 'Alba', and *C. fragilis* with bright blue flowers.

They flower in succession, *C. fragilis* carrying its blooms in one great burst in August, followed by *isophylla* which will bloom until frost.

Very nearly hardy, both are ideal for seasonal use in hanging baskets throughout the warmer months.

With us on the North Wales coast, both can be grown in the open garden, so that one can dig up and divide pieces as required for basket or window box use.

Good compost and regular feeding are necessary if they are to keep up their display. They tend to exhaust the compost and will deteriorate if not returned to the open garden for a spell (where the climate is sufficiently mild). Otherwise they may be renewed by dividing into small pieces, potting in John Innes No. 3 and keeping under glass. Several pieces may go into a 5- or 7-inch pot and should be fed with a suitable liquid manure every 10 days to encourage them to increase.

The plants can later be transferred to accompany other genera in hanging baskets. Otherwise they may be potted individually into 5-inch pots, placed in cradles of galvanised wire and suspended from the ceiling of an entrance porch or loggia. They may also be slipped into ornamental pot holders on the wall to form attractive cascades of silver or blue.

Other plants for hanging baskets include the pendulous varieties of tuberous-rooted begonia such as 'Golden Showers', 'Mrs Bilkey', 'Lena' and 'Meteor', ruffled petunias and—showiest and cheapest of all, dwarf nasturtiums of the 'Tom Thumb' type.

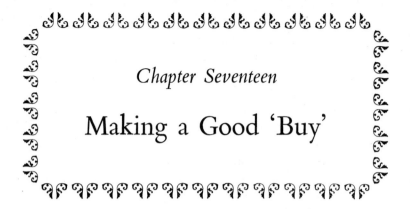

Chapter Seventeen

Making a Good 'Buy'

Particularly when buying plants for summer display in window boxes and containers does it pay to be careful. Too many spindly, poor plants are offered too early in the summer. Too often they stand, without proper watering, in the over-heated atmosphere of a multiple store, are taken home and planted out without proper hardening off and, although well planted, duly 'puddled in', and kept well watered, receive such a shock that they either fail to recover or are so set back that flowering is delayed, and they remain poor plants all their lives.

First, it is important to know just what you want to buy. This means working out several colour schemes in advance and being prepared to substitute if you cannot get just what you want.

Do not purchase plants too early. Mid-May is soon enough for the hardier types such as antirrhinums, penstemons and stocks to go out in most districts. Asters and petunias should be left until the end of May and really tender subjects such as nemesia, zinnia, *Phlox drummondii* and nicotiana should wait until all frost danger is past—about the second week in June in most districts.

Occasional bargains in the way of dwarf azaleas and rhododendrons can sometimes be bought from the multiple stores and some of the bulbs sold by these stores are satisfactory, but it is as well to give them a miss when purchasing bedding plants. If you have a good local nursery go there well in advance—about Easter

is not too soon—ask for their list, work out the quantities of
plants you need and give your order. If you leave it until planting
time most of the boxes of the self-coloured strains will have gone
and you will have to settle either for 'mixed' colours or for half
a dozen here and a dozen there of whatever summer bedding
plants happen to be left.

The same thing applies to autumn planting of wallflowers or
Brompton stocks. Orders should go in at the beginning of
September, otherwise you may be disappointed.

Give your order in good time to a reliable nursery, is the wisest
rule, and do not rely on impulse buying.

In some city districts, however, there may be no nearby nurseries, or you may have left ordering too late, or you may decide
to shop around for unusual varieties or for a kind of plant your
nursery may have been unable to supply.

Local flower shops and market stalls are good alternative
sources of supply, and so long as you know what you are looking
for you should not go far wrong. Be prepared to shop around,
though, and do not accept second-rate plants.

Hardening off is most important. You can tell at once whether
plants have been properly hardened off before sale by the colour
of the leaves. Deep green, thick-textured leaves are what you are
looking for.

See that the plants are short-jointed and sturdy and with leaves
of the right colour. Such plants will have been grown cool with
adequate soil and space in which to develop.

Avoid plants that have been overcrowded. Antirrhinums,
stocks and petunias should not be set more than four dozen in
a standard seed tray $14\frac{1}{2}$ inches long by 9 inches wide. Smaller
plants, such as lobelia, may have 60 to a tray without being
cramped. Large plants like zinnias and nicotianas or dwarf dahlias
should not be packed more than 30 to a tray. See, too, that the
trays are at least $2\frac{1}{2}$ inches deep so that there will have been plenty
of room for the roots to develop properly. Plants grown under
these conditions may be more expensive to buy, but the results
will more than justify the extra cost.

With stocks, be sure to buy only the 'hundred per cent double' strains, as single-flowered sorts among the doubles in a window box can spoil the display. When buying antirrhinums, pick the rust-resistant strains, and with petunias go for the vigorous F_1 hybrids. When buying asters, turn down those that show any signs of flagging or that have brown marks near the soil level, denoting aster wilt. Such plants will usually die before flowering.

Beware of buying bedding plants in flower. If they are in flower too soon, they will have been brought on too fast or grown in poor soil, and so will be spindly and never do well. Be particularly careful when buying nemesias to be sure that you get sturdy, well-branched plants. Too many nemesias are thin and spindly, sold too soon and never giving good results.

Plants of a different category such as pansies, violas and primulas are often sold in flower, and this is no detriment. With pansies and violas go for healthy looking, bushy plants of the colours you want. With primulas look for young stock. Beware of small, poor leaves and lack of vigour due to being propagated from pieces of worn-out crown, or being lifted from nursery rows after several seasons of neglect, without division. The best results will be obtained from plants sown the previous May.

When buying pelargoniums, pick the compact, short-jointed plants that have been grown in individual containers, and look for the deep leaf colour that indicates they have been well hardened off. Dahlias and begonias, too, will give better results if they have been individually grown.

With bulbs and shrubs it always pays to go to a reliable supplier —a nursery or garden centre. In gardening it is safe to say that the cheapest seldom gives the best results. It is worth spending just a little more for a satisfying result.

The list of suppliers appended here is intended as a *general* guide. There are many more, equally good, but I have tried to indicate where most gardening needs may be met and to cover as many areas of Britain as possible. Gardeners in the United States, New Zealand, Australia, Southern Africa and other countries overseas can gain some guidance from the advertisements in their gardening magazines. As a rule it is only the *genuine* suppliers who advertise in the specialist magazines.

GARDEN AND NURSERY SUPPLIERS

Barrels and tubs—strawberry barrels, etc.
Barrel House, Chapel Porth, St Agnes, Cornwall.
Kingston Cooperage, 45A Acre Rd., Kingston-upon-Thames,
Surrey.

Bulbs
Carters Tested Seeds Ltd., Raynes Park, London, S.W.20.

Camellias
Haskins Bros. Ltd., Tricketts Cross, Ferndown, Dorset.
Hillier and Sons, Winchester, Hants.
Treseder's Nurseries Ltd., The Nurseries, Truro, Cornwall.
W. C. Wicks Ltd., Specialist Growers, Lambley, Nottingham.

Chrysanthemums—dwarf varieties
Orpington Nurseries, Rocky Lane, Gatton Park, Reigate,
Surrey.

Clematis
Fisk's Clematis Nursery, Westleton, Saxmundham, Suffolk.
Pennell and Sons Ltd., 312 High Street, Lincoln.

Fibre Glass Window Box and Containers (antique reproductions)
Verine Products & Co., Folly Faunts House, Goldhanger,
Maldon, Essex.

Foliage Plants
Rochford's House Plants, Hoddesdon, Hertfordshire (wholesale only. Look out for their label in the window of your local
supplier.)

Fuchsias
Idehurst Nursery, Wisborough Green, Billingshurst, Sussex.
Wills Fuchsia Nursery, 285 Winchester Road, Southampton.

Garden Centres
William Wood and Sons Ltd., Bath Road (A4), Taplow, Maidenhead, Berks.

Plant Centre
Bodnant Gardens, Taly-Cafn, Denbighshire.

Hardy Heaths
Maxwell and Beale Ltd., Naked Cross Nurseries, Corfe Mullen, Wimborne, Dorset.

Hardy Plants
Sunningdale Nurseries, Windlesham, Surrey.

Herbs
E. & A. Evetts, Ashfields Herb Nursery, Hinstock, Market Drayton, Salop.

Hydrangeas, outdoor varieties only
Michael Haworth-Booth, Farall Nurseries, Haslemere, Surrey.
Sunningdale Nurseries, Windlesham, Surrey.
W. C. Wicks, Ltd., Specialist Growers, Lambley, Nottingham.

Levington Compost, Fisons Peat
Queries on the treatment of pests and diseases also to Fisons Garden Advisory Service, Harston, Cambridge.

Mild Area Plants
Treseder's Nurseries Ltd., The Nurseries, Truro, Cornwall.

Miniature Bulbs
Barr House, Bishops Hull, Taunton, Somerset.

Pelargoniums and Geraniums
Ayton, Anthony C. Ltd., Constables, Kibbles Lane, Southborough, Kent.
Clifton Geranium Nurseries, Cherry Orchard Road, Chichester, Sussex.

Pots and Tubs in reproduction stoneware—also green-bronze pottery containers
W. Teakle and Co. Ltd., 26 Denmark St., Wokingham, Berks.

Pots and Tubs etc.
Patio Design, 4 Ladbroke Grove, Holland Park Avenue, London, W.11.

Propagators
Autogrow Ltd., Quay Road, Blyth, Northumberland.
Humex Ltd., 5 High Road, Byfleet, Surrey.

Rhododendrons and Azaleas
Hillier and Sons, Winchester, Hants.
Hydon Nurseries Ltd., Hydon Heath, Godalming, Surrey.
Sunningdale Nurseries, Windlesham, Surrey.

Rock Garden Plants
W. E. Th. Ingwersen Ltd., Gravetye, East Grinstead, Sussex.
Reginald Kaye Ltd., Silverdale, Carnforth, Lancs.

Roses
David Austin Ltd, Albrighton, Wolverhampton.
Edwin Murrell, Portland Nurseries, Shrewsbury, Salop.
C. Gregory and Son Ltd., The Rose Gardens, Chilwell, Nottingham.

Seedsmen
Samuel Dobie and Son Ltd., 11 Grosvenor Street, Chester, Cheshire.
Fogwills Ltd., Friary Street, Guildford, Surrey.
Sutton and Sons Ltd., The Royal Seed Establishment, Reading, Berks.
G. Telkamp and Sons Ltd., 148 Fenchurch Street, London, E.C.3 (for Dutch Hybrids).
Thompson and Morgan (Ipswich) Ltd., London Road, Ipswich, Suffolk (for rare seeds and novelties).

Shade Plants
   Newlake Gardens, Copthorne, Crawley, Sussex.

Sundries
   E. J. Woodman and Sons (Pinner), Ltd., 19–25 High Street, Pinner, Middlesex.
   E. J. Woollard Ltd., 146 High Street, Waltham Cross, Herts.

Trees and Shrubs
   Burkwood and Skipworth Ltd., Lane End Nurseries, Hockley Lane, Elstead, near Godalming, Surrey.
   Hillier and Sons, Winchester, Hants.
   Sunningdale Nurseries, Windlesham, Surrey.

Water-lilies and Aquatics
   L. Haig and Co. Ltd., The Aquatic Nurseries, Newdigate, Surrey.
   Perry's Hardy Plant Farm, Enfield, Middlesex.

Chapter Eighteen

Everyman's Plant List for Window Boxes and Containers

African Marigold—see Tagetes.

Agapanthus 'Headbourne Hybrids' (Blue Lily of the Nile) Evergreen perennial. Height $2\frac{1}{2}$ feet, spread 2 feet. Heads of blue flowers, July–August. Tub. Protect in winter in cold districts.

Ageratum Half-hardy annual. 6 inches–$1\frac{1}{2}$ feet high. Fluffy flowers usually blue, occasionally heliotrope or white, July–September. Window box, trough and tub. Plant out in June.

Anaphalis triplinervis (Everlasting) Herbaceous perennial. Height $1\frac{1}{2}$ feet, spread 1 foot. Foliage silvery. Flowers paper white in a corymb. Flowering August onwards. Window box.

Antirrhinum Herbaceous perennial. Treat as annual or biennial. Sow in late August–September for May flowering, or February–March in heat for July flowering. Various colours. Window box, trough, etc.

Aubrieta deltoides Carpeting perennial. Window box, front row trailing subject. Purple, lavender and rose, March–April.

Aucuba japonica Scarlet-berried shrub for tubs. Height 5–8 feet, spread to 7 feet, but can be pruned to size.

Azalea Lime-free soil. Evergreen or deciduous. Yellow, orange, red or pink, mostly May flowering. Window box or pots.

Bay—see Laurus.

Begonia rex Foliage plant. Tender. Pot grown in greenhouse. Window box, trough.

Begonia semperflorens Fibrous-rooted, half-hardy annual, 6–9 inches tall. Raise in heat February–March. Pink, red or white flowers. Window box or trough.

Begonia, tuberous rooted Raise from tubers in spring. $1\frac{1}{2}$ feet. Various colours, single and double flowers. Window box. Cascade type suitable for hanging baskets.

Bergenia Herbaceous perennial. Good foliage and early flowers, February–April, pink, red and white. Height 1–2 feet, spread 2 feet. Large leaves turning crimson in winter. Window box, tub.

Buxus sempervirens Evergreen box. Shrubby. Tub. Stands clipping.

B.s. 'Suffruticosa' Dwarf. Window box.

Camellia japonica and × *williamsii* cultivars Evergreen shrubs. Beautiful flowers in spring, pink, red or white, and handsome foliage. Height up to 6 feet in tub, and spread 3–4 feet. Lime-free soil. Tub and pot.

Campanula Several species and varieties of this perennial suitable for window box, trough, pot and sink use, especially *C. arvatica, carpatica, C. turbinata, cochlearifolia, isophylla* (tender), *lactiflora* 'Pouffe', *portenschlagiana, poscharskyana*, all blue-flowered from June or early July. Height 6–12 inches.

Castor-oil plant—see Fatsia.

Ceanothus dentatus 'Russellianus' Evergreen shrub. Height 6–8 feet in pot, and spread 4 feet. Blue flowers, May–June. Prune after flowering if necessary. Large pot or tub.

Ceratostigma plumbaginoides Herbaceous perennial. Height 1½ feet, spreading. Bright blue flowers, July–October, crimson leaves. Window box and trough.

Chamaecyparis—dwarf cultivars.

Cheiranthus cheiri (Wallflower) Treat as biennial. Sow under glass or in open in May. Transplant twice. Plant in window boxes or troughs about a foot apart in October. Early flowering cultivars are especially useful in mild areas. Various colours, flowering March–May.

Choisya ternata (Mexican orange blossom) Evergreen shrub. Height 4–6 feet, spread 5–6 feet. Scented white flowers in April–May. Glossy foliage. Pot or tub.

Chrysanthemum—dwarf cultivars such as Otley Koreans and pompons, flower September–October, various colours, except blue. Winter the stools indoors, and raise from cuttings taken in heat early in the year. Window box, pot and trough.

Citrus Oranges, lemons and grapefruit. Fine pot subjects in New Zealand, Australia, Southern Africa, Florida and Mediterranean region. Tender elsewhere and should be taken indoors from mid-September until May. Evergreen.

Clematis Climbers for tubs and pots, some evergreen. Train up cylinders of plastic mesh. Flowers from April–September, according to species. Various colours, single and double flowers.

Coleus Tender foliage plant, 1–1½ feet high. Pot grown in greenhouse. Leaves brightly coloured and patterned. Summer window box or trough.

Corylus avellana 'Contorta' Twisted hazel. Height 8 feet in pot. Picturesque deciduous tree for terrace, patio or roof-garden. Catkins in early spring.

Crown Imperial—see *Fritillaria imperialis*.

Elaeagnus pungens 'Maculata' Evergreen, yellow-variegated shrub. Height 5 feet, spread 5–6 feet. Tub.

Euonymus fortunei 'Variegatus' Slow-growing evergreen, leaves white variegated, sometimes tinged pink. Window box or tub.

'Everlasting'—see Anaphalis.

Fatsia japonica (Castor-oil plant) Evergreen, large, palmate leaves. Height 5–8 feet, spread 6–10 feet. Some shade preferred. Mild areas or winter shelter. Pot or tub.

Forget-me-not—see Myosotis.

French Marigold—see Tagetes.

Fritillaria imperialis (Crown imperial) Impressive bulbous subjects for spring, with their tufted cluster of hanging orange or yellow bells on 2-foot stalks. Plant in autumn. Pot or tub.

Fuchsia Tender shrub. Pot grown. Height $1\frac{1}{2}$–2 feet as bush, 3 feet as standard in pot. Flowers purple, red and white in various combinations. Window box, trough, tub, pot. Winter in frost-free place and plant out in May.

'Geranium'—see Pelargonium.

Geranium endressii Low-growing herbaceous plant. Pink flowers all summer. Trough or tub.

Geranium grandiflorum Low-growing herbaceous plant. Blue flowers June and September. Trough or tub.

Hebe (*Veronica*) 'Violet Queen' and various *elliptica* hybrids and forms make excellent container plants for mild areas. 1–3 feet. Stands clipping. Evergreen. Bottle-brush flowers in white, mauve, purple or pink. Window box or tub.

Heliotrope Half-hardy plant. Height $1\frac{1}{2}$–2 feet. Violet flowers. Sweet scent. Pot grown. Window box or trough.

Hibiscus Hardy (*H. syriacus*) and tender (*H. rosa-sinensis*) shrubs. Tub or pot. Blue, red, pink or white flowers, late summer. Tender species must have winter cover in cool latitudes. Especially suitable for Florida, Honolulu, Mexico, New Zealand (North Island), Australia and South Africa.

Holly—see Ilex.

Hyacinth Scented bulbs. Early flowering, March. Plant in autumn. Window box, trough, pot and bowl.

Hydrangea macrophylla Deciduous shrub. Height 3–4 feet in tubs, spread 2–4 feet. Flower colours white, pink, red, blue, violet. Treat with blueing powder or commercial alum dissolved in water—2 tablespoons of the latter to 1 gallon of water, giving the solution fortnightly through spring and summer to produce blue flowers. It should be freely applied. Window box, tub and pot.

Ilex aquifolium (Holly) 'Golden King' and 'Silver Queen'. Foliage variegated. Both male and female plants necessary for berries. Height 3–4 feet, width 3 feet in tubs.

Ipomoea—see Pharbitis.

Jasminum nudiflorum (yellow winter jasmine), *primulinus* (tender, yellow, spring flowering) and *officinale* (white, scented, summer flowering). Train the first two species which are wall shrubs on trellis on wall or at back of pot. *Jasminum officinale*, however, is a true climber and should have a Netlon cylinder encircling the pot on which to climb.

Laurus nobilis (Bay) Height in tubs 3–5 feet. Spread 2½–4 feet. Aromatic, glossy, evergreen foliage. Tub or pot. Give shelter in winter.

Laurustinus—see Viburnum.

Lavandula spica nana Dwarf lavender—*alba* (white), 'Hidcote' (purple). Window box, trough, pot and bowl.

Lemon verbena—see Lippia.

Lilac—see Syringa.

Lilium Make good pot plants. They do well in camellia compost. Varieties for pots and tubs are *L. auratum, henryi, regale* and *speciosum,* as well as the new vigorous American hybrids. See Chapter Fifteen.

Lippia citriodora (Lemon verbena) Semi-tender. Deciduous shrub. Height in pot 6–8 feet. Lemon scented, pale purple flowers. Winter cover essential.

Lobelia erinus Tender perennial treated as annual. Blue flowers. Sow in heat in February–March. Plant out in May. Window box, trough, tub and hanging basket.

Lobularia maritima (Sweet alyssum) Annual. Fragrant dwarf bedding plant. White or mauve. Sow in boxes. Plant out in May. Window box, trough, etc.

Matthiola incana (Stock) Biennial. Various colours. Sow outdoors in May or June. Brompton stock, spring flowering. East Lothian stock for late summer flowering, from March sowing in heat.

Mexican orange blossom—see Choisya.

Morning glory—see Pharbitis.

Myosotis alpestris (Forget-me-not) Spring colour. Sow in May out of doors. Transplant. 'Blue Ball' 6 inches, 'Royal Blue' 1 foot. Window box or trough.

Myrtus communis Tender. Fragrant, evergreen shrub. Place against wall in mild counties. Otherwise give winter shelter. Height 4–6 feet. Tub or pot.

Nerium oleander Tender evergreen shrub. Yellow, white or pink flowers, June onwards. Height in tub 4–6 feet. Put out of doors in May. Take into greenhouse late September. Tub. Suitable warm climates and southern hemisphere gardens.

Nicotiana (Tobacco plant) Tender. Treat as annual. Height 2 feet, spread 1–1½ feet. Flowers white, pink, deep red, yellow-green, scented, June–September. Raise in heat in pots or boxes. Plant out in June. Tub or trough.

Nymphaea (Water-lily) Tubs or tanks in water. See Chapter Fourteen for varieties.

Osmarea × *burkwoodii* Evergreen shrub. White, sweetly scented flowers in spring. Height in tub 3–4 feet, spread 4 feet. Tub.

Pansy—see Viola.

Passiflora caerulea Semi-hardy passion flower. Flowers mainly blue, from late June onwards. Climber for tub. Protect in winter in cold areas.

Pelargonium ('Geranium') Half-hardy perennial. Sub-shrubby. Red, pink, crimson, white and vermilion. Ivy-leafed trailing varieties and upright zonals and regals. Excellent for window boxes, troughs, pots and hanging baskets. Pot grown. Propagate by cuttings. Winter under glass. Plant out in June.

Periwinkle—see Vinca.

Petunia Treat as annual. Tender. Purple, red, pink, white, blue and combinations of these colours. Sow in heat in early spring. Plant out in June. Some cultivars have scent. Window box, trough, pot, urn, hanging basket.

Pharbitis hederacea (*Ipomoea*) (Morning Glory) Tender summer climber. Glorious blue flowers. Raise from seed. Pot or tub. Train up Netlon panels or cylinders.

'*Polyanthus*' (Polyanthus Primula) Sow seeds under glass in February–March. Harden off in cold frame. Transplant twice. Plant in boxes and troughs September for flowering the following spring. All colours. Can be divided in autumn.

Punica granatum (Pomegranate) Tender shrub, for mild areas, or can be grown elsewhere with winter protection. Height 3–4 feet in tub. Flowers red, June–September. Tub or pot. *P. g. nana* is a dwarf form to about 1 foot.

Rhododendron Dwarf cultivars and azaleas suitable for window box or tub. Lime-free soil essential. Flowers all colours, mainly in spring.

Roses Miniature roses suitable for window boxes or pots. Height 9–18 in.

Salvia Scarlet salvia. *Salvia patens*, 2 feet, blue, flowers late summer. Tender. Raise in heat. Plant out in window box or trough, June.

Senecio cineraria (syn. *S. maritima*) Sub-shrub. Tender. Grey foliage plant, leaves much cut and dissected. Height 1–2 feet. Pot grown. Increase by cuttings. Plant out in May. Window box, trough, tub, urn.

Stock—see Matthiola.

Sweet Alyssum—see Lobularia.

Syringa vulgaris (Lilac) Half standards are useful for tub cultivation, reaching 6-8 feet in height and bearing their sweetly scented flowers in May. Good double cultivars are 'Charles Joly' red, 'Katherine Havemayer' blue-lavender, and 'Madame Lemoine' white. These are more likely to be obtainable as small standards than are the newer cultivars.

Tagetes erecta (African Marigold) Annual. Tender. All shades of orange and yellow. Sow under glass. Plant out in June. Dwarf strains suitable for window boxes, troughs and bowls.

Tagetes petula (French Marigold) Annual. Yellow, brown, deep red. Tender. Height to $1\frac{1}{2}$ feet. Sow under glass. Plant out June. Window box and pot.

Thymus serpyllum (Alpine thyme) Sinks and troughs.

Tobacco plant—see Nicotiana.

Tulip Bulbous plant. Plant November. Early doubles and rock-garden hybrids suitable for window boxes. Taller sorts suitable for pots and bowls.

Verbena rigida (syn. *V. venosa*) Herbaceous perennial used for bedding. Height to 2 feet. Mauve-purple flowers. Pot or box grown. Plant out in May. Window box and trough. Tuberous roots can be kept over winter like dahlias.

Veronica—see Hebe.

Viburnum carlesii Scented deciduous shrub for tubs. Height 3 feet. Flowers white, in spring.

Viburnum tinus (Laurustinus) Evergreen shrub, winter blossom, pink-white. Height in tub 5 feet. Tub.

Vinca (Periwinkle) Prostrate evergreen trailers (some with variegated foliage). Flowers usually blue, but also white, reddish and pink. Window box, tub and urn.

Viola (*including Pansy*) Height 4–9 inches. Treat as annual. Increased by cuttings or seeds. Window box, trough, pot.

Wallflower—see Cheiranthus.

Water-lily—see Nymphaea.

Wisteria floribunda or *sinensis* Climbing shrubs. Can be trained as standards. Pot or tub. Lilac flowers, May, and occasionally through summer.

Yucca filamentosa Evergreen shrub. Handsome spiky leaves, tall spires, cream lily flowers when mature in July. Large tub.

PART THREE

Window box and container
gardening in warmer climates

Chapter Nineteen

International Window Boxes

Similar types of plant are used for window box cultivation throughout most of the world—from the cool temperate zones with their British-type climate, through the warm temperate areas such as Madeira, the Canary Islands, Tasmania, and parts of North Island, New Zealand, to the Mediterranean climatic zones of Southern France, Spain, Italy and Greece, California, Victoria and Southern New South Wales in Australia and Cape Province in South Africa, to the tropical climates of Natal, Florida, Northern New South Wales and Queensland and the islands of Hawaii and Fiji.

In all these places may be seen the familiar petunias, lobelia and pansies of British window boxes, joined by *Impatiens sultanii*, the ubiquitous 'busy Lizzie', the main difference being that as the hotter zones are reached these subjects are used for spring displays and not for summer, their places being taken during the hotter months by such drought resisters as 'geraniums' and free-flowering succulents of the zygocactus type.

Many areas with cold winters such as Switzerland, Germany, much of the United States and even Scandinavia, experience hot summer temperatures so here, too, window box gardeners tend to rely on geraniums for summer display. Only in hot climates with much humidity in the atmosphere are commonly used foliage subjects such as those the British gardeners regard as indoor pot plants—the purple and striped zebrina and tradescantias, the crotons with their leaves multi-coloured like Joseph's coat and the handsome *Begonia rex.*

Technically, of course, these foliage beauties could be used equally well in British window boxes during the summer months but, being so vulnerable to the weather, their use might be considered wasteful and they are not often so employed. There is, however, a case for their inclusion among flowering subjects to enhance the display. One sometimes sees *Senecio cineraria*, with its handsome silver leaves, in this context, but some of the beautifully marked begonias and coleus might also be included. They would combine well with pink and crimson tuberous begonias, with cherry and pink fibrous begonias and blue ageratum. Like the tuberous-rooted begonias, they would be seen at their best in partial shade.

Pelargoniums—both zonal and ivy-leaf—are among the very best plants for hot, dry positions. This is probably why we see them in Spanish window boxes and pots to the exclusion of almost all other plants.

In those regions of southern Africa which experience hot, dry summers, much use is made of the leafier cacti and succulents, and this is a vogue which might be followed with advantage by window box gardeners in other countries with similar climates.

Most succulents need an airy, sunny position, although some of the crassulas, scarlet kalanchoe, senecios and sedums will tolerate shade. Drainage of the compost must, however, be good. On the other hand, the compost should not be too poor. In South Africa, it has been found that a mixture containing well-rotted garden compost, peat and sand is ideal. No great depth of soil is needed, and so the succulents will do well in shallow boxes for which it might otherwise be difficult to find suitable occupants. They dislike frost, and in regions with hot summers and cold winter nights (like the Greek islands, Cape Province and the Transvaal) they should be given warm, sheltered positions. In really cold places they should be pot grown, as they will need to be brought indoors during the winter. Overhead drip is fatal to succulents, so they should be planted only in window boxes protected by a good overhang of roof.

Zygocactus and epiphyllums are among the showiest genera, with their cascading fleshy green leaves and brilliant fuchsia-like flowers. *Crassula portulaca* 'Pink Joy' makes good, bushy plants that give a fine display. These may be associated with the low-growing *Kalanchoe blossfeldiana* with its scarlet flowers, rat's-tail cactus to droop over the front of the box, *Rochea coccinea* with its crimson posies, and one or two small plants of the dramatically shaped opuntia (prickly pear).

Euphorbia splendens, the scarlet-flowered crown of thorns, is also suitable, as are most members of the brightly coloured mesembryanthemum family (vygies) of which lampranthus and drosanthemum are perhaps the best. The annual portulacas and dwarf zinnias with their bright, pretty flowers are suitable for seasonal use and can be discarded as they go over.

Small shrubs such as the scarlet-fruited capsicums, *Senecio galpinii* with its fluffy orange flowers, and the trailing *Lantana selloviana* (syn. *Lippia montevidensis*) are also good.

For late summer use, *Sedum spectabile* with its fresh green foliage and flattened heads of dusky pink makes an attractive follow-on to earlier flowers.

Drying out is always a problem, and to deal with this and meet the watering need during weekend absences from home, the capillary watering system now widely used in greenhouses might be adapted to window box needs.

Working on the principle of capillary attraction, the plants, in individual pots, should stand in a plastic trough chosen to fit the window box and filled with moist sand. The moisture in the sand can be maintained by piped water from a central ball tank or individual glug bottles bracketed on the wall in a slightly higher position to the side of the window box.

Gardeners in the U.K., who might like to experiment with this system, can purchase glug bottles or tanks from Humex Ltd. (see p. 127 for address).

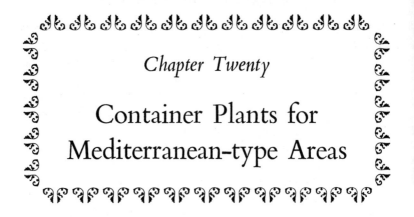

Chapter Twenty

Container Plants for Mediterranean-type Areas

Much of the foregoing information and many ideas will be applicable to container gardening all over the world. For favourable Mediterranean-type climates (such as those of California, New Zealand's North Island, Southern Australia, and Cape Province, South Africa, as well as in the Atlantic islands, the coast of Portugal and the region around the Mediterranean sea) there are additional delightful plants to consider.

Hippeastrums—known to many of us more familiarly as amaryllis—are among the most satisfactory of the bulbous subjects for pots.

Having very large bulbs, the hippeastrums should be given at least a 7-inch individual pot. They will thrive in any good garden soil and will benefit from the inclusion of moist peat if you can get it. If not, use fibrous loam; John Innes No. 2 compost is also good.

Plant the bulbs in well-crocked pots with their necks just above soil level in August and keep them well watered. When the flower buds emerge give the plants a teaspoonful of concentrated liquid fertiliser and repeat again when the flower opens. Water them well throughout the growing season and about mid-summer prick in a little well-balanced general flower fertiliser.

Dry off the plants in May, even if the leaves are still green, and allow the bulbs to rest before starting to water again in August.

Repot every second year in August, separating the bulbs which will have increased and replanting them in individual pots.

Hippeastrums are ideal bulbs for sub-tropical latitudes and for the southern hemisphere. They do particularly well in a moist climate such as that of Madeira, Natal and the Auckland area of New Zealand.

Lilies make just as good pot plants in more favourable climates as they do in the indifferent British weather, but in warmer climates virus diseases and botrytis fungus cause even more trouble. South Africa, fortunately, is remarkably free from these troubles, and in much of the United States they have been less common since the older strains of lilies made way for the new vigorous Jan de Graaff hybrids.

The tiger lily, *Lilium tigrinum*, is particularly prone to virus attack, so it should either be avoided or kept right apart from other lilies. Aphids are the chief culprits in spreading disease to healthy plants, so these should be kept at bay by spraying. A tip that can be borrowed from British cottage gardens is the regular emptying of the suds from the washing-up bowl over the lily pots—yet another reason for sticking to soap and eschewing detergents!

Lilies need some sunshine, but the pots should be placed where they will receive shade during the heat of the afternoon in hot climates.

Plant in March and April in the southern hemisphere, crocking the pots, as described in Chapter Fifteen, setting the bulbs about 4–6 inches below the surface and spacing the bulbs 1–2 feet apart. Fill in at once with good topsoil mixed with compost and soak it deeply, covering with a mulch of peat-moss or compost to keep it cool. It is helpful to grow small perennials or shallow-rooted annuals in the pots with the lilies to shade their roots. The bright blue *Salvia patens*, violas such as 'Mrs Pickering' and 'Maggie Mott', ageratum or lobelia are attractive, or one might plant frilly pink and white petunias or blue petunias according to the colour of the lily blooms.

Lilies may be raised easily from seed in warm climates. Sow the seed in trays or in the open ground, spacing it about ½ inch apart. Keep the seedlings well watered and give them light dressings of compost during the growing period. Leave them where they are until the bulblets are ½ inch in diameter. They can then be moved to nursery beds or planted directly into the pots in which they will flower. Many lilies flower in their second year. The seed may be sown in spring or autumn. Either way, growth will not start until the spring. The quickest lilies to flower from seed are the Madonna lily (*Lilium candidum*), regal lily (*L. regale*) and the hybrids of the trumpet and *umbellatum* sections. The *auratum* and *speciosum* hybrids take longer to germinate, the seed often not starting into growth until the second spring.

Coloured arums—zantedeschia species such as the pink *Z. rehmannii*, and yellow arums, *Z. angustiloba* and *melanoleuca tropicalis* species and varieties, make rewarding pot plants. The tubers should be planted about mid-August in the southern hemisphere. They should be set about 2 inches below the surface and 6 inches apart.

These arums must be kept well watered during the summer months, and they must have full sun or they will not bloom properly. Good drainage is essential, but any good garden soil with the addition of well-rotted manure or compost will suit them. Divide the tubers and repot every second year to keep them blooming freely.

Bougainvilleas are usually seen as climbers but they can also be used with great success as pot or tub plants for the patio. They enjoy the reflected heat from walls and paving and with their roots restricted by the container will flower more freely.

In New Zealand in particular, and other areas with comparatively cool summer climates, although 'Scarlet O'Hara' and the purple 'Magnifica' will flower almost anywhere in the garden, many of the choicer varieties will flower better when container grown. By curbing their greedy roots and standing the pots or tubs where they can enjoy reflected heat from the wall they will flower much more freely. Overlong whippy shoots should be cut back to a flower bud, the aim being to make lowish mounded plants that will become fountains of colour.

Good cultivars to try are the well-known 'Killie Campbell' (terra-cotta), 'Temple Fire' (rich red), 'Pink Champagne' (pale pink), 'Doubloon' (amber), and 'Mrs Butt' (rose-red) and 'Hawaiian White'.

A newer cultivar with cream-margined foliage is exceptionally decorative. It is as well to note that its name, 'Cream Delight', refers to the leaf variegation as the flowers (bracts) are rosy red.

Hibiscus, those symbols of welcome and delight in tropical islands, do well in tubs and in their newer cultivars, are among the showiest of all shrubs. Like the bougainvilleas, they do well in patio conditions as they need plenty of sun. They need plenty of moisture, too, and rich feeding, so their compost should contain a good proportion of peat (moistened before use) and a generous ration of well-rotted animal manure.

Specially attractive are the double rose 'Mrs Horton', double yellow 'Eldorado', the single yellow 'Californian Gold' with a deep red eye, and the large, pink, single 'Agnes Gault'.

Oleanders do well. See Chapter Eighteen for growing hints, but remember that they will seldom need the protection required under British conditions.

Acacia, known to Australians as 'wattle' and to much of the rest of the world as 'mimosa', has many delightful species that are suitable for growing in tubs.

Valuable for their early flowers, the container-grown acacias should be placed near the house where their fragrant sunny flowers can be enjoyed on warm days in winter and early spring.

Best known is *Acacia baileyana* with its beautiful, fern-like, silver-blue foliage and lemon-yellow flower puffs. Reaching a height of 6–8 feet in a tub, this species is easily kept manageable by the pinching out of unwanted shoots as growth begins in spring.

A useful small grower is *Acacia fimbriata* (syn. *A. prominens*), the 'Golden Rain Wattle', with graceful weeping branches and fluffy yellow-duckling flowers in early spring.

The dwarf *A. glandulicarpa* (listed by nurserymen in Australia and New Zealand), is sometimes available and appreciates hot, dry patio conditions. Reaching only 3 feet it makes an attractive plant for a low pot, with its crinkly-edged leaves and abundance of rich golden flowers.

Acacias grow in the wild in poor, dry, sunbaked soil. They should *never* be given manure, and need sharp drainage. Grow them in ordinary garden soil and prune them back immediately after flowering for the best results.

Azaleas and scented rhododendrons do extremely well in California, Hawaii, North Island, New Zealand and in Natal. When pot grown they should be removed from the terrace or patio after flowering and plunged in their pots to the rim in a cool, shady spot until the autumn. It is important to see that they do not dry out. Soaked peat heaped over the pots after watering will help to retain the moisture.

Chapter Twenty-one

Pot Plants in the Tropics

Much of central and southern America, most of Africa, the northern half of Australia, the whole of India, New Guinea and Malaysia have a climate with an average temperature of over 21 °C (70 °F). The nearer one gets to the equator, the more humid and steamy the air becomes, and luxuriant tropical jungle or rain forest conditions predominate.

In such conditions organic matter used in potting composts rots too quickly. This means that the soil becomes hard and caked with watering, so it is necessary to incorporate really coarse fibre and grit to keep the compost open.

A good potting compost for hot countries consists of:

4 parts fibrous loam (consisting of the top few inches of soil from old grassland)
2 parts coarse fibre (chopped grass roots or the bases of palm leaves well chopped)
1 part broken brick and charcoal (all parts by bulk)
plus one handful of bonemeal or guano to 4 gallons of compost.

Plants will grow in such a mixture for several years without repotting.

Evaporation is rapid in unglazed pots, so plastic pots are preferable where they can be obtained. Where porous pots are used, the inside should be coated with wax or painted with waterproof paint.

Wooden containers should be of hard, resistant timber such as teak, on account of borers and termites.

Metal containers (painted cans and drums) must stand in the shade as they become too hot in the sun.

In hot countries plant growth seldom stops, so it is important to keep up an adequate supply of nutriment by administering liquid feed every two or three weeks.

Tap water may contain mineral deposits which would build up harmfully over the months, so it pays wherever possible to collect rain water and to use it for watering the pot plants.

Plants with coloured leaves such as the caladiums, coleus, begonias and fittonias are attractive when their pots are interspersed with pots of the fern-like selaginella. The decorative leaves of tradescantia and zebrina also look well, but the plants grow so quickly that they will need frequent replanting. *Rhoeo discolor* is slower in growth, and with its green and purple leaves will do well in shade. For a sunny spot, the purple leaves of the pink-flowered *Setcreasea purpurea* will give a similar effect.

Flowering plants such as *Eucharis grandiflora* with its waxy white flowers and broad, dark green leaves will do well in a hot, moist climate. It needs a shady position.

Impatiens sultanii, grown as a tender annual in British gardens, makes a colourful pot plant with its never-ending sequence of pink, orange and scarlet flowers. Like the eucharis in really hot climates, it needs shady, moist conditions.

The lovely blue agapanthus, lily of the Nile, so well known to gardeners in Cape Province for its rippling tide of Christmas flowers, will do well in full sun provided it gets adequate water during the growing season.

Aphelandra squarrosa, with its showy yellow cockscombs of flower and white-veined greenery, will grow and flower well in a pot, as will crossandra and ixora.

African violet (*Saintpaulia*), achimenes and the glorious gloxinias (*Sinningia*) deserve protection from rain and sun for the sake of their velvety leaves and beautifully coloured flowers, so a shady verandah suits them best.

Begonias make fine pot plants but they, too, need shade from full sun and the dwarf, free-flowering *B. semperflorens* cultivars are colourful and pretty with their clusters of golden-centred flowers in crimson, pink, scarlet, white or gold.

Many of these small plants do better in pots than they would in the open borders in climates where the soil is constantly leached by the rain and baked hard by the sun until few nutriments remain.

Bougainvilleas, hibiscus and oleander (see previous chapter) can be grown as tall flowering subjects, while jacaranda and the feathery *Grevillea robusta* may be grown for foliage beauty along with small palms, cycads and dwarf bamboos such as *Nandina domestica*.

Index

153

Colour schemes, 34
Coltness dahlias, 48
Compost, 29–32, 108, 142, 149; *et passim*
Conifers, 82, 84
Conifers, dwarf, 41, 52–4, 109, 114
Construction, of window boxes, 21–8
Containers, 81 ff; siting, 86–92; types available, 81–5; watering, 85–6, 93–4, 98
Convolvulus, 44–5
Convolvulus varieties: 'Royal Ensign', 44
Convolvulus mauritanicus, 97
Convolvulus minor, 63, 70
Cornflower, 61
Corylus avellana 'Contorta', 91, 132
Crassula portulaca 'Pink Joy', 143
Crassulas, 142
Crocuses, 22, 34, 51, 60, 61
Crocus ancyrensis, 52
Crocus ancyrensis 'Golden Bunch', 110
Crocus chrysanthus, 34, 52
Crocus sieberi, 52
Crocus tomasinianus, 52
Crocus tomasinianus 'White Purple', 52
Crossandra, 150
Cutting back and dead heading, 64
Cuttings, 67–69
Cyananthus integer, 60
Cyananthus microphyllus, 60
Cycads, 151
Cyclamen, 72
Cyclamen orbiculatum, 59
Cytisus kewensis, 37

Daffodils, 34, 35
Daffodils, varieties: 'Angel's Tears', 38; 'February Gold', 35; 'March Sunshine', 35; 'Mrs W. P. Milner', 38; 'Peeping Tom', 35; 'Rosy Trumpet', 38
Dahlias, 14, 46–7, 66, 74, 123, 124
Dahlias, Collarette, 46
Dahlias, Coltness, 47
Dahlias, Coltness Gem, 47, 48
Daisies, 39, 69
Damping off, 66
Datura suaveolens, 97
Delphiniums, 15
Delphinium nudicaule, 59
Design, of window boxes, 21–8
Dianthus deltoides, 59

Dianthus freynii, 59, 109
Dianthus neglectus, 59
Dinocap, 66, 102
Diseases and pests, 66, 102
Dithane, 102
Drainage, of window boxes, 14, 22, 24, 29
Drosanthemum, 143

Edraianthus pumili, 110
Elaeagnus pungens 'Maculata', 98, 132
Epiphyllums, 143
Erica carnea, 19, 50
Erica carnea, cultivars: 'Springwood', 52; 'Springwood Pink', 52; 'Winter Beauty', 52
Erica × darleyensis 'A. T. Johnson', 51
Erica mediterranea 'W. T. Rackliff', 50
Erinus alpinus 'Mrs Charles Boyle', 109
Erinus 'Dr Haenaele', 59
Erythronium dens-canis, 59
Erythronium johnsonii, 59
Erythronium revolutum, 59
Eucalyptus, 83
Eucharis grandiflora, 150
Euonymus fortunei 'Variegatus', 132
Euonymus radicans 'Silver Queen', 51, 52
Euphorbia splendens, 143

Farrer's harebell poppy, 60
Fatsia japonica, 88, 89, 132
Fertilisers, 30–1, 63
Fisons Liquinure, 32
Fisons Plantgrow, 32, 42, 62
Fittonias, 150
Flags, yellow, 105
Flax, New Zealand, 82
Forget-me-nots, 38, 69, 135
Forget-me-not, water, 105
Forsythia, 114
French marigolds, 14, 31, 32, 33, 44, 65, 70, 73, 76, 137
Fritillaria imperialis, 132
Fritillaria meleagris, 110
Fruit, 99 ff.
Fuchsias, 16, 31, 42, 46, 68, 73, 98, 120, 125, 132
Fuchsias, varieties: 'Alice Hofman', 42; 'Cascade', 120; 'Dusky Rose', 120; 'Lena', 42; 'Margaret', 42; 'Marinka',

Fuchsias, varieties—*contd.*
42, 120; 'Red Spider', 120; 'Rose of
Castile', 42; 'White Spider', 120
Fuji cherry, 95

Galanthus elwesii, 52
Genista pilosa, 109
Gentian, spring, 59
Gentiana acaulis, 59
Gentiana angulosa, 60
Gentiana cachemirica, 59
Gentiana excisa, 59
Gentiana farreri, 60
Gentiana gracilipes, 60
Gentiana 'Kidbrooke Seedling', 60
Gentiana × *macaulayi* 'Well's Variety',
59
Gentiana sino-ornata, 59
Gentiana verna, 109
Geranium argenteum, 60
Geranium dalmaticum, 60
Geranium endressii, 132
Geranium endressii 'A. T. Johnson', 74
Geranium farreri, 109
Geranium grandiflorum, 113, 132
Geranium napuligerum, 109
Geranium sanguineum lancastriense, 60
Geraniums, *see* Pelargoniums
Ginkgo, 114
Gloxinias, 150
Grape hyacinths, 34, 35
Grapefruit, 131
Greenfly, 66, 102, 145
Grevillea robusta, 151
Ground-covering plants, 33
Gutters, for window boxes, 16, 21
Gymnocalycium, 58
Gypsophila 'Rosy Veil', 75
Gypsophila 'Fratensis', 109

Hanging baskets, 43, 118–21
Heaths, 14, 69, 98, 126
Heaths, Cape, 51
Heaths, winter, 14, 16, 22, 24, 35, 50–1,
64
Heaths, cultivars: 'Elsie Purnell', 98;
'Gold Haze', 98; 'Robert Chapman',
98
Hebe (Veronica), 16, 45, 49
Hebe speciosa, 45
Hebe 'Violet Queen', 49, 133
Hedera 'Silver Queen', 34
Heliotrope, 42–3, 68, 71, 73, 75, 133

Heliotropes, varieties: 'Gratton Park',
43; 'President Garfield', 43; 'Princess
Marina', 43
Hepaticas, 60
Herbs, 16, 54–5, 126
Hibiscus, 82, 133, 147, 151
Hibiscus, cultivars: 'Agnes Gault',
147; 'Californian Gold', 147; 'Eldo-
rado', 147; 'Mrs Horton', 147
Hibiscus rosa-sinensis, 133
Hibiscus syriacus, 133
Hippeastrums, 144–5
Holly, 133
Hottonia palustris, 105
Houstonia caerulea, 109
Humex Pottagator, 67, 72
Hyacinths, 24, 34–5, 64, 133
Hyacinths, Roman, 38
Hyacinths, Cynthella, 38
Hyacinths, varieties: 'Anne Marie', 35;
'City of Haarlem', 35; 'Jan Bos', 35;
'Myosotis', 35
Hydrangeas, 14, 15, 24, 30, 41–2, 64, 65,
66, 67, 68, 74, 126
Hydrangeas, cultivar 'Vulcan', 41, 42
Hydrangea macrophylla, 133

Ilex aquifolium, 133
Impatiens, 71, 76–7
Impatiens sultanii, 141, 150
Ipomoea, 136
Ipomoea hederacea, 84
Irises, 60, 105
Iris cristata, 60
Iris danfordiae, 52
Iris histrioides, 59
Iris lacustris, 60, 110
Iris laevigata 'Rose Queen', 105
Iris reticulata 'Clairette', 35
Ivies, 26, 34, 51–2, 64, 83, 85
Ixora, 150

Jacaranda, 151
Jasmine, 84, 113
Jasmine, winter, 49, 114, 133
Jasminum nudiflorum, 49, 114, 133
Jasminum officinale, 133
Jasminum primulinus, 133
Jeffersonia dubia, 60
Jiffy pots, 57, 71
John Innes potting composts, 30, 31, 33,
70, *et passim*
Juniperus chinensis, 114